# It's Time to Rock the Boat

## A Call to God's People to Rise Up and Preach a Confrontational Gospel

**Other Books by Michael L. Brown**

*From Holy Laughter to Holy Fire:*
*America on the Edge of Revival*

*Israel's Divine Healer*
(Studies in Old Testament Biblical Theology)

*Our Hands Are Stained With Blood:*
*The Tragic Story of the "Church" and the Jewish People*

*Whatever Happened to the Power of God:*
*Is the Charismatic Church Slain in the Spirit*
*or Down for the Count?*

*How Saved Are We?*

*The End of the American Gospel Enterprise*

*Compassionate Father or Consuming Fire?*
*Who Is the God of the Old Testament?*

*Let No One Deceive You:*
*Confronting the Critics of Revival*

For information on ICN Ministries, or for a listing of
other books and tapes by Michael L. Brown, write to:

**ICN Ministries**
**P.O. Box 36157**
**Pensacola, FL 32506**
**Phone: (850) 458-6424**
**FAX: (850) 458-1828**
**E-mail: RevivalNow@msn.com**

# It's Time to Rock the Boat

## A Call to God's People to Rise Up and Preach a Confrontational Gospel

**By**
**Michael L. Brown**

**Destiny Image® Publishers, Inc.**
**P.O. Box 310**
**Shippensburg, PA 17257-0310**

"Speaking to the Purposes of God for This Generation
and for the Generations to Come"

ISBN 1-56043-106-7

For Worldwide Distribution
Printed in the U.S.A.

Fifth Printing:   1997          Sixth Printing:   1997

This book and all other Destiny Image, Revival Press,
and Treasure House books are available
at Christian bookstores and distributors worldwide.

For a U.S. bookstore nearest you, call **1-800-722-6774**.
For more information on foreign distributors, call **717-532-3040**.
Or reach us on the Internet: **http://www.reapernet.com**

# Contents

# Preface
# (Giant vs. the Fanatic)

On January 31, 1991, after months of urging from my wife, I wrote a letter to the Vice-President of Consumer Affairs for Giant Food Inc., commending their fine chain of grocery stores for their cleanliness, service, product selection and competitive prices. In particular, I thanked the Vice-President for her consumer's rights ads that had been airing on the radio. But we too had something to air—and it was not a radio ad! It was a serious grievance that we, and many of our friends and co-workers, shared: Must we be exposed to sexual smut at every single check-out counter? To quote from my letter:

> There is simply no way to avoid the bombardment. From the front pages of *Cosmopolitan* to *National Enquirer*, we are confronted with racy pictures of half-naked women and explicit details of the latest sexual adventures, deviant practices, and scandalous affairs of the rich and famous. This cannot possibly contribute to the kind of upright, conscientious atmosphere that you seem to portray in your advertising.

We have spoken to a good number of people in the community about this issue and every one agrees: the women feel violated, the men feel polluted, and the children are being miserably poisoned. Must we be subjected to such degrading material every time we do our shopping?

I understand fully the extremely lucrative nature of the magazine check-out area. In fact, I have been informed that it yields the greatest amount of dollars per square foot in all of your stores. But economics is not the only factor! Customer satisfaction and good morals must rank high on your list of priorities as well. Otherwise, why not sell *Playboy*, *Penthouse*, and X-rated videos—if making money is all that matters? If you would simply look at the range of offensive materials offered at the check-out counters (see the enclosed sampling of one day's representative dirt), I think you would agree that they are not in the public's best interest.

Ideally, it would be great if the magazines in question were removed from Giant entirely. However, I realize at this time that this is not realistic. I would urge you instead to move these materials to the general magazine rack. That way those who want to buy them can still do so by walking over to that particular area (just like they buy everything else in the store!), while the rest of us would not have to be confronted with all the filth.

If, however, economics *is* the deciding factor, then you should take into account that in my position as Dean of a widely attended Montgomery County Bible School, I am in contact with a large representation of churches and pastors. All those I have spoken to have shared this sentiment: We will take our business to whichever major food store will remove the objectionable magazines and tabloids from the check-out counters. We trust that the voice of multiplied thousands of customers will not go unheeded. Of course, should Giant respond favorably to our request, then I would strongly encourage our associates to bring *all* of their business to your stores. I believe that Giant's favorable actions with regard to this request would be a newsworthy item. (Needless to say, Giant's refusal to act would also be a newsworthy item.)

Thank you for your attention in this matter. I look forward to your prompt response.

Also enclosed was one day's representative sampling of magazine and tabloid cover lines (these are just a few of the examples we listed): Sensual Treats to Enjoy Alone; Diary of an Affair—A Tale of Lust and Betrayal; When Happily Marrieds Are Secretly Unfaithful; My Husband Met Her at Church—Why Even Good Men Stray; Men We Lust For—Men We Marry; Woman Caught in the Grip of Love, Sex and Alcohol; Oprah Was Pregnant at 14—Her Sizzling Romance With a Married Man; Grand Ole Opry—Sex Scandal—Preacher Caught With Mistress; Mistress Mom Tells All; Romantic Revenge—The Heady Pleasure of Getting Even.

At this point you may be wondering: Why pick on one chain of stores? Don't most grocery stores display this trash at the check-out counters? Well, Giant Food was not just any chain of stores. It was one of the biggest companies in the Maryland, Virginia and Washington D.C. area, it had a fine reputation for being a *family-oriented* store, and in every one of its more than 150 locations, a large sign listing "The Consumer's Bill of Rights" hung for all to see. We were convinced that it was right to act.

Our reasons for targeting this issue were also simple: (a) If we didn't speak up, things would only get worse; (b) The

Bible commands us to keep ourselves unspotted by the world, and relocating this degrading material would help us to stay unpolluted; (c) It was an unnecessary assault on the family (including impressionable little children); (d) Somebody had to rock the boat somewhere!

The Vice-President immediately called me back and, after a long talk, agreed to set up a major meeting. This meeting, held two months later with senior officials of the company, as well as with my wife Nancy and another pastor, led to a second meeting. At this next meeting, I had the pleasure of gently confronting the marketing agents of Hearst Corporation, *publishers of both Good Housekeeping and Cosmopolitan*, with their sin: It was anti-family, anti-moral and anti-God to promote adultery and immorality.

Of course, they thought I was being unfair. "After all," they said, "we must be doing a lot of things right. *Cosmopolitan* is the nation's seventh best-selling publication." But they forgot to mention that *Penthouse* (!) was number six, and that *National Enquirer* and *Star* were numbers three and four. (No wonder our country is so messed up!)

The Board of Directors of Giant deliberated about the issue and *decided to do nothing*. We promised them that we would do something. We would circulate petitions to the local churches, asking the members to urge Giant to *relocate* (not remove) these objectionable materials. Otherwise we would take our business to the stores that *would* relocate this trash. We also decided to contact one county-wide newspaper with a circulation of about 42,000, the

*Montgomery Journal.* Little did we realize what would happen.

The *Journal* editors expressed a real desire to cover the story, but we were in for quite a surprise: It was front-page coverage in the Monday, August 5, edition! And, yes, that meant a front-page picture too, bearing this caption: "Why isn't this man smiling?" On page three, the whole story was written up with the headline reading: "Pursuing a Giant Conversion." It became some of the hottest news in the area.

The *Journal* article contained quotes from the ACLU (they somehow managed to accuse us of censorship) and from Helen Gurley Brown, editor of *Cosmopolitan* (obviously she wasn't happy), and within just a couple of hours, the story was picked up *nationally* by AP News Services. The phones at our school offices were almost ringing off the hook: Secular radio stations wanted interviews on live call-in programs, news agencies were asking for short interviews over the phone, a local TV station wanted a spot done on their 6 o'clock News live, while another TV network was sending a camera crew for an interview at our offices. And this was just the first day!

Over the next few weeks, the story was covered (or criticized) on countless radio and TV news spots; we were attacked in the lead article of the *Washington Post* Business Section ("Giant Resists a Pressure Group"); our campaign was given feature coverage in the *Baltimore Sun* (they apologized for not putting us on the front page, but explained that the Soviet Union was collapsing!). There were appearances on several live call-in radio shows (they were hot and heavy, although the first host ultimately came out on our side), as well as on several live TV news or talk shows. One friend even heard a total stranger cursing me out while checking out of one store: "Who does this Mike Brown [expletives deleted] think he is, telling us what we can and cannot read!" (Of course, we weren't telling *anyone* what they could and couldn't read.) The story was also carried nationally on Christian radio by Family News in Focus. And all this furor was over a simple request to remove what the media called "supermarket smut" from the check-out counters and relocate it to another part of the store!

Letters to the Editor, as well as editorials, also began to appear, and friends would send them to my attention. One editorial began: "Self-Appointed Sentry Looks Out for Public Taste. Thumbs Down to Michael Brown...." (I countered this with a letter that they published entitled: "Thumbs Down to Those Who Promote Smut.") Some readers sided with us. Others were really hot: "I smell a fanatic.... Thumbs down to Brown for his delirious attempts to save society from what he somehow assumes we find offensive." Rudolph Pyatt, in his business column for the *Washington Post*, was quite articulate, referring to our "threats [such as petitioning or possibly picketing], which when stripped of their apparent righteous indignation, bear a striking similarity to the tactics employed by more undesirable elements in protection rackets"! (Of course, the *Post* published my response to this article too.)

My schedule was turned topsy-turvy. Things were unbelievably hectic. But almost every day, I was able to discuss the miserable moral condition of our nation with news people or with neighbors. "Twenty years ago, did we bombard our children and families with sexual trash *at the grocery stores*?" We were now being held "captive at the counter," as one newspaper put it. What had become of our moral standards?

But there was one more surprise to come. A Jewish columnist for the *Montgomery Journal* read about our campaign and said to himself, "This doesn't sound Jewish!" (I was identified in many articles as a "Messianic Jew.") So he wrote a column attacking *our religious beliefs*, entitled: "Why are some Christians in the county posing as Jews?" It was a miserable, unfair write-up, put together hastily to meet a deadline. But it quoted from some of our material, and actually preached the gospel unintentionally!

I called the paper and asked if there was a forum through which I could respond. They gave me my own column! There, I had the incredible privilege of laying out the claims of Jesus the Jewish Messiah, without spending a dime for publicity. Not only that, but the *Journal* received many other letters from offended readers (mainly Jewish believers), and they published these letters together with my article. We had almost an entire newspaper page to preach the gospel, especially to our fellow Jews! *And all of it started because my wife urged me to take a stand against ungodly material at the grocery check-out counters.* This is the good news.

The bad news is, although Giant removed the tabloids (but no magazines, not even *Cosmopolitan*) from just one aisle in each of their stores (the so-called "No Candy Aisle" for parents who don't want their kids to be tempted by candy while waiting in line), they refused to do anything else. *We could not give them a strong enough reason for action*, for the really bad news is we were only able to rally several churches behind us. After much prayer and many calls and letters from our office, when we could collect only a few thousand signatures (instead of the 10,000 we wanted), we dropped our efforts. We realized that, without a united church, we would be fighting a losing battle. I was obviously not the man to bring these pastors together, even over such a simple issue. And for some of them, even signing a petition was considered too radical a thing to do, while others simply didn't know me well enough to join in the battle. (I do not judge any of these ministers at all; I'm only reporting to you what happened.)

But one crucial lesson was learned: Whenever the people of God, led and equipped by His Spirit, confront sin and unrighteousness in the society, it will always provide a platform for the preaching of the gospel message. *This book is a biblical challenge to each and every one of us to rise up and preach a confrontational gospel.* It is a call to rock the boat!

Chapter One was written in the fall of 1991, shortly after the events described in this Preface. Other chapters soon followed, although most of the material was written at the end of 1992 and the beginning of 1993.

When I was completing the book, I noticed two things: I had quoted especially frequently from William Booth, the founder of the Salvation Army, and the theme of martyrdom was surprisingly common throughout the chapters.

Could there be a lesson? Is it time for a new kind of radical army to arise, just as fiery and dedicated to winning souls at any cost as were the original Salvation Army workers? And could it be that some of us will be called on to lay down our lives for the truth *in this generation, right here in America*? May God give us grace to stand firm.

Once again, it is my special joy to thank Leonard and Martha Ravenhill, dear saints well into their 80's, but always moving me on with their brokenhearted intercession and love; my co-workers John and Joanne Cava, for helping to birth these themes in prayer; Don Nori, President of Destiny Image, for urging me to write this book *now* after seeing the first few chapters this past fall; and my faithful companion and dear wife Nancy, for her uncompromising integrity and loyalty. And above all, I delight in thanking my best friend Jesus, who never fails or falls short. Joseph Caryl (1602-1673) said it so well: "He is the best friend at all times, and the only friend at sometimes." Thank God for such a wonderful Savior!

*Our religious neutrality is threatened whenever someone we know well takes spiritual commitment seriously and refuses any longer to play hide-and-seek and touch-and-go with the living God.*

Carl F. H. Henry

*It is possible within the provisions of redemptive grace to enter into a state of union with Christ so perfect that the world will instinctively react toward us exactly as it did toward Him in the days of His flesh.*

A.W. Tozer

*The world may frown—Satan may rage—but go on! Live for God. May I die in the field of battle.*

James B. Taylor

*If their houses were on fire, thou wouldst run and help them; and wilt thou not help them when their souls are almost at the fire of hell?*

Richard Baxter

*Oh! if we had more love to you, we would tell you more about hell. They do not love you who do not warn you, poor hell-deserving sinners. Oh! remember that love warns.*

Robert Murray M'Cheyne

# Chapter One

# The Confrontational Gospel

God's people are called to rock the boat. We are not called to coexist with this sinful society. We are called to confront it. We are not called to a life of comfort. We are called to a life of conflict. Following Jesus does not mean catering to our selfish desires. It means crucifying them. Are we ready to walk in the Savior's footsteps?

Remember, the world hated Jesus. He made people uncomfortable. He exposed sin. He rebuked unrighteousness. He would not compromise. He would not hold back. *And He was nailed to a cross by a godless world.* Why should it be any different for us?

He was rejected; we want to be respected. He was regarded as radical; we want to be recognized as reasonable. He was accused of having demons; we are acclaimed for having degrees. He was put out; we long to be taken in.

He put no stock in the praise of man; we thrive on it. Is it any wonder we make so little impact here for Him?

Why was John the Baptist beheaded? Why was Stephen stoned? Why was Paul persecuted? Was it because they shared the four spiritual laws with their friends? Was it because they told those friends that they could have a better life if they would only ask Jesus in? Was it because they promised prosperity and plenty to those who would tithe to their ministries? No. *It was because they preached a confrontational gospel.* That is the only gospel there is!

Look at John 16:5-11. Jesus was speaking of the ministry of the Spirit. Soon Jesus would be leaving His disciples—but not as orphans. He would send the Holy Spirit, and the Spirit would take over the work. In fact, Jesus clearly said that it was *better* for Him to leave so the Spirit of God could come. What exactly would the Spirit do?

> When He comes, He will convict the world of guilt in regard to sin and righteousness and judgment: in regard to sin, because men do not believe in Me; in regard to righteousness, because I am going to the Father, where you can see Me no longer; and in regard to judgment, because the prince of this world now stands condemned. (John 16:8-11)

Those are amazing words! The Holy Spirit came to bring glory to the Son. *He begins by convicting the world of its guilt in regard to sin, righteousness and judgment.* How often do we hear about that? How often do we ask God to send His Spirit to bring conviction and to expose sin? Yet that is the very thing that points people to Jesus, since without conviction there is no conversion, and without conviction the cross makes no sense. As Andrew Bonar observed:

> In bringing a soul to the Savior, the Holy Spirit invariably [or at least, commonly!] leads it to very deep consciousness of sin.

*That* is a shattering experience for proud, independent flesh.

Samuel Logan Brengle, the fervent Salvation Army soul winner, said:

> Men used to fall as though cut down in battle under the preaching of Wesley, Whitefield, Finney and others. And while there may not be the same physical manifestations at all times, there will surely be the same opening of eyes to spiritual things, breaking of hearts and piercing of consciences. The Spirit under the preaching of a man filled with the Holy Ghost will often come upon a congregation like a wind, and heads will droop, eyes will brim with tears, and hearts will break under convicting power.... [This] ought to be a common sight under the preaching of all servants of God; for what are we sent for but to convict men of their sin and their need, and by the power of the Spirit to lead them to the Savior?
>
> And not only will there be conviction under such preaching, but generally, if not always, there will be conversion and sanctification.

Consider the ministry of John, the forerunner of Jesus. His baptism of repentance was not an abstract spiritual mission. His preaching dealt with everyday life and delved into everyday sins. To the repentant tax collectors John said, "Don't collect any more than you are required to" (Luke 3:13). To the contrite soldiers he said, "Don't extort money and don't accuse people falsely—be content with your pay"

(Luke 3:14). To the religious hypocrites he said, "You brood of vipers! Produce fruit worthy of repentance. Put no trust in your illustrious spiritual lineage" (see Matt. 3:7-10). In other words, don't say, "I'm Assembly of God, or Word of Faith, or Baptist, or Messianic Jewish, or Apostolic...." God is not impressed with titles. He's looking for the fruit of changed lives!

What did John tell Herod? Did he tell the king, "Only believe"? Did he say, "You're the king. I'll change my message for you"? No! John rebuked Herod for all his evils, especially for his adulterous marriage (see Luke 3:19). In God's eyes it was no marriage at all. (How many of *today's* "marriages," blessed by the Church and sanctioned by the clergy, are also adulterous in His eyes?) Herod the king was a sinner. The big shot leader needed to repent. John called him to account. *That* is part of the preaching of the gospel.

But John was not just a preacher of judgment. His purpose in coming into the world was absolutely clear: "I myself did not know Him, but the reason I came baptizing with water was that He might be revealed to Israel" (John 1:31). John the Baptist came to make Jesus known to Israel! Like the Holy Spirit, John's whole goal was to point people to the Son. And like the Holy Spirit, he began by exposing sin. *Then*—naked, exposed and guilty—the people cried out in repentance. *Then* they were ready for the Savior. Like the Israelites of old, they cried out only when they found themselves snake-bitten and dying. "Heal us, O Lord!" (See Numbers 21:4-9.)

John the Baptist had the greatest ministry of any prophet under the Old Covenant. He was called to prepare the way for the Lord. He did it by preaching repentance. He did it by rocking the boat. Nothing has changed today—except our message and our method! We think we know better. We think we are more sophisticated. We think we have reached a higher plane. But have we?

When John preached, the people cried out, "What shall we do?" Today we are lucky if we can persuade people to come to the altar to pray a two-minute prayer. When John preached, with no hype, no Hollywood, no P.R. and no P.A., huge crowds came. Today, with mass media at our fingertips and sophisticated salesmanship up our sleeves, we can hardly fill an auditorium. And when we do manage to pack the house, we hardly make an impact on the population of Heaven. Less than 15 percent of the unsaved who respond to the altar call end up walking with the Lord!

Just think: With no synagogues working together and with no advance organizing committees, all Jerusalem and Judea came to hear John preach his uncompromising message. Today it takes enormous networking efforts and co-ordination schemes to gather 20,000 souls. Then, after all that, most of those who come are already saved! And what do they come to hear? A pep talk! A positive message! The gospel equivalent of a motivational sales pitch! We have *not* improved on the ministry of John.

What about the ministry of Stephen? Have we improved on that? Stephen was "a man full of God's grace and power, [and he] did great wonders and miraculous signs among the people. *Opposition arose*, however..." (Acts 6:8-9). Why? His testimony was a threat and his message was a menace—to the religious establishment. But when they sought to oppose him, "they could not stand up against his wisdom or the Spirit by whom he spoke" (Acts 6:10). When his accusers brought him forth to be examined:

> All who were sitting in the Sanhedrin looked intently at Stephen, and they saw that his face was like the face of an angel. (Acts 6:15)

Here was a man without compromise, a man overflowing with God. Here was a man wholly on fire, a burning torch in the Master's hand. *And he sealed his life by confronting religious hypocrisy.* That was how he testified for Jesus! He rebuked his people Israel for being stiff-necked, for resisting the Holy Spirit, for persecuting the prophets, for betraying and murdering the Lord, and for disobeying the law. His message made the leaders furious.

> …[They] gnashed their teeth at him. But Stephen, *full of the Holy Spirit*, looked up to heaven and saw the glory of God, and Jesus standing at the right hand of God. "Look," he said, "I see heaven open and the Son of Man standing at the right hand of God." (Acts 7:54-56)

What a scene! This man was caught up and consumed, impassioned and empowered. This man knew God's heart, and he preached God's heart—rebuking and reproving his obstinate people for rejecting the Redeemer. And the glory of God appeared.

It was more than the people could bear. In a mad frenzy, "they covered their ears and, yelling at the top of their voices, they all rushed at him, dragged him out of the city and began to stone him" (Acts 7:57-58), but not before the dying saint committed his spirit to the Lord and interceded for his assailants. "And Saul was there, giving approval to his death" (Acts 8:1). Soon Saul, the arch persecutor of the people of God, was one of them too. Could it be that he could not shake Stephen's sermon? (It was really the sermon of the Spirit.) Could it be that Stephen's dying prayer availed for Saul? "Lord, do not hold this sin against them" (Acts 7:60), or against him?

A message of confrontation produced a miracle of conversion. The world has never been the same since. Holy conviction overtook Saul!

What was *his* message like? When Paul (Saul) was in Caesarea, Felix and his Jewish wife Drusilla sent for him and "listened to him as he spoke about faith in Christ Jesus" (Acts 24:24). But Paul didn't just say, "Believe in Jesus!" Paul "discoursed on righteousness, self-control and the judgment to come" (Acts 24:25). *That* was part of Paul's message on "faith in Christ Jesus"! How many evangelistic sermons do we hear that deal with topics like "righteousness, self-control and the judgment to come"? Could it be that Paul knew something about gospel preaching that we don't know?

> As Paul discoursed...Felix was afraid and said, "That's enough for now! You may leave. When I find it convenient, I will send for you." (Acts 24:25)

The preaching of Paul the prisoner made the governor nervous! His message got under Felix's skin. Paul had chosen his subject wisely; historians tell us that Felix was living in adultery. When he met Drusilla, she was married to another. But Felix, overwhelmed by her beauty, took her *unlawfully* to be his wife. (Actually, she became his third wife.) When Paul "discoursed on righteousness, self-control and the judgment to come," it was more than Felix could take. That's why he became afraid and said, "That's enough for now!"

John's wilderness preaching so incensed King Herod that he put John in prison. Stephen's message so enraged the Sanhedrin that this elite group of scholars became a raging mob. And Paul's too-close-for-comfort discourse shook up the governor and his wife.

Here were three men, filled with the Spirit, declaring a Spirit-filled word. It ultimately cost them their lives. Their message stirred up so much opposition that they were *killed* because of what they *said*. (Stop and chew on *that* for a moment.) *They preached a confrontational gospel.* Will we follow their lead?

*Give me one hundred men who fear nothing but sin, and desire nothing but God, and I will shake the world.*

John Wesley

*Oh, for an utter abandonment to the Spirit! ... Whenever, in any period of the Church's history, a little company has sprung up plastic and pliable in the hands of the divine Spirit, **then a new Pentecost has dawned.***

James Alexander Stewart

*You come against me with sword and spear and javelin, but I come against you in the name of the Lord Almighty, the God of the armies of Israel, whom you have defied. ... All those gathered here will know that it is not by sword or spear that the Lord saves; for the battle is the Lord's, and He will give all of you into our hands. (Addressing Goliath and the Philistines.)*

David, 1 Sam. 17:45,47

*Alack [alas] for thee, it's no more to me than a straw. (His answer to a man who confronted him with a brandished sword.)*

George Fox

*If God were not my friend, Satan would not be so much my enemy.*

Thomas Brooks

*If you leave people as you found them, God is not speaking by you. If you are not making people mad or glad, there is something amiss with your ministry. If there is not a war on, it's a bad job for you.*

Smith Wigglesworth

# Chapter Two

# The Lord's Troublemakers

The Lord is not looking for troublemakers—for the sake of trouble alone. The Word is perfectly clear:

Make it your ambition to lead a quiet life, to mind your own business and to work with your hands...so that your daily life may win the respect of outsiders.... (1 Thess. 4:11-12)

Make every effort to live in peace with all men...." (Heb. 12:14)

I urge, then, first of all, that requests, prayers, intercession and thanksgiving be made for everyone—for kings and all those in authority, that we may live peaceful and quiet lives in all godliness and holiness. (1 Tim. 2:1-2)

Blessed are the peacemakers, for they will be called sons of God. (Matt. 5:9)

No, the Lord has not called us to suffer for foolishness or laziness, or for offensive and obnoxious behavior. Peter instructed:

If you suffer, it should not be as a murderer or thief or any other kind of criminal, or even as a meddler. (1 Pet. 4:15)

There is nothing glorious about suffering for our sins!

But of this we can be sure: If we follow Jesus, we *will* suffer and we *will* get into trouble. It's inevitable!

> To this you were called, because Christ suffered for you, leaving you an example, that you should follow in His steps. (1 Pet. 2:21)

And what an example He left!

> If the head of the house has been called Beelzebub, how much more the members of his household! (Matt. 10:25b)

(Remember how the world treated Jesus, and then hear His words "how much more"!)

The Son of God was absolutely blameless and totally perfect in character and conduct, yet the world mocked and maligned Him, rejected and ridiculed Him, cursed and crucified Him—and it does so to this very day. Did Jesus know what He was talking about when He warned us?

> Woe to you when all men speak well of you, for that is how their fathers treated the false prophets. (Luke 6:26)

Why should we fare any better than Jeremiah or Paul?

> All men will hate you because of Me, but he who stands firm to the end will be saved. (Matt. 10:22)

*Hate* is quite a strong word! Does it mean anything to us that all the apostles, save one, died a martyr's death?

Look at the pattern in the Book of Acts. Speaking of apostolic preaching, Arthur Wallis wrote:

> Such preaching, by making indifference impossible, sets the hearers in one of two camps. It is calculated to produce a revival or a riot.

Apostolic words and actions create quite a stir!

In Lystra, the crowd first wanted to *sacrifice* to Paul after a great miracle was performed; moments later they *stoned* him. (See Acts 14:8-20.) Did anyone need to ask Paul exactly what he meant when he taught, a short time later: "We must go through many hardships to enter the kingdom of God" (Acts 14:22)?

At Philippi, Paul confronted the spirit of divination in a slave girl. The next thing he knew, he and Silas were brought before the magistrates:

> ...These men are Jews, and are *throwing our city into an uproar* by advocating customs unlawful for us Romans to accept or practice. (Acts 16:20-21)

All they were doing was preaching Jesus and driving out demons. But what could be more confrontational than that?

> The crowd joined in the attack against Paul and Silas, and the magistrates ordered them to be stripped and beaten. (Acts 16:22)

But the story's not over yet. About midnight, as they prayed and sang hymns—their feet bound with fetters, their bodies racked with pain, but their spirits soaring in the heavenlies—God sent an earthquake that shook the whole jail. It's almost too much to believe, yet it happened. The gospel caused *everything* to quake. The magistrates then came in person to the prison, appeased these apostolic men (Paul and Silas were Roman citizens) and asked them to *please leave the city.* (See Acts 16:23-39.)

Then, at Thessalonica, Paul went into the synagogue, as was his custom, and explained and proved from the Scriptures that Jesus was the Messiah (Acts 17:1-4). How civil and well-mannered!

> But the Jews were jealous; so they rounded up some bad characters from the marketplace, formed a mob and *started a riot in the city*.... (Acts 17:5)—

all because Paul was preaching the gospel! This time there were no miracles (as at Lystra) and no demons cast out (as at Philippi); there was just some good public Bible teaching. *Still there was a riot.*

> But when they did not find them [Paul and Silas], they dragged Jason and some other brothers before the city officials, shouting: "These men who have caused trouble all over the world have now come here." (Acts 17:6)

By this time the believers were getting quite a reputation! The controversy was over one thing, or should we say one Person: *Jesus*. (Read Acts 17:7!) Some of the Thessalonian Jews were so angry with this Jewish message about a Jewish Messiah being preached by a Jewish apostle that they also agitated and stirred up the crowds against Paul in Berea (Acts 17:13). (Take note of that word *crowds*: The gospel draws attention.)

Are you starting to get the picture? One reason that Scripture urges us to mind our own business and to keep a good reputation with outsiders is *the gospel itself creates enough trouble of its own.* Even when we try to stay out of trouble, some demonic troublemakers will come along; that is, if we are preaching the message of the cross and living in the power of the resurrection. Something is bound to get stirred up then!

In Ephesus "God did extraordinary miracles through Paul, so that even handkerchiefs and aprons that had touched him were taken to the sick, and their illnesses were cured and the evil spirits left them" (Acts 19:11-12). Even demons acknowledged the power of Jesus and His servant Paul (Acts 19:13-16).

> ...They [the people] were all seized with fear, and the name of the Lord Jesus was held in high honor. Many of those who believed now came and openly confessed their evil deeds. A number who had practiced sorcery brought their scrolls together and burned them publicly.... In this way the word of the Lord spread widely and grew in power. (Acts 19:17-20)

This was revival, without a doubt. But a riot was not far off.

"About that time there arose a great disturbance about the Way" (Acts 19:23) because idol sales were being threatened, and so the silversmiths, whose very livelihood was at stake, "were furious and began shouting: 'Great is Artemis of the Ephesians!' *Soon the whole city was in an uproar...*" (Acts 19:28-29). Why should things be any different today?

Listen again to these words from Acts: "These men are Jews, and are throwing our city into an uproar...These men who have caused trouble all over the world have now come here...Soon the whole city was in an uproar."

When Paul finally made it to Jerusalem:

> ...some Jews from the province of Asia saw Paul at the temple. They stirred up the whole crowd and seized him, shouting, "Men of Israel, help us! *This is the man* who teaches all men everywhere against our people and our law and this place...." ... *The whole city was aroused*, and the

people came running from all directions. Seizing Paul, they dragged him from the temple, and immediately the gates were shut. While they were trying to kill him, news reached the commander of the Roman troops that *the whole city of Jerusalem was in an uproar.* (Acts 21:27-28; 30-31)

Paul hadn't even opened his mouth. He didn't say a single word!

When Paul reached the steps, the violence of the mob was so great he had to be carried by the soldiers. (Acts 21:35)

Then it was time for Paul to share his testimony. As they heard him speaking in their native tongue, "they became very quiet" (Acts 22:1-2). That is, until he shared his life commission:

Then the Lord said to me, "Go; I will send you far away to the Gentiles."...Then they raised their voices and shouted, "Rid the earth of him! He's not fit to live!" (Acts 22:21-22)

These religious men literally went wild, "shouting and throwing off their cloaks and flinging dust into the air" (Acts 22:23). *A testimony of true spiritual transformation will always drive the establishment crazy.*

Jewish believers, this is the kind of opposition you can expect when you declare Yeshua to ultra-Orthodox Jews. Former Muslims who are now saved, this is the kind of trouble you'll run into when you proclaim Christ the Lord to serious Muslims. Catholics who have been born from above, this is the kind of attack you'll experience when you preach the new birth to staunch Catholic traditionalists. (Just try it in Mexico or Guatemala if you don't believe me!) Even "open-minded, peace-loving" Hindus go berserk when their religious stranglehold is threatened by the living words of living witnesses who testify to the truth of the only living God.

*The Lord certainly has His troublemakers in the earth, pulling down strongholds of darkness, stirring up the fury of the devil, confronting sin without fear, boldly proclaiming the good news.* As Leonard Ravenhill stated, "A man needs to be anointed only one hour in his entire life, and he can change the whole world." How powerful God's uprooting is!

Some of us would do well to pray Samson's prayer: "O Sovereign Lord, remember me. O God, please strengthen me just once more, and let me with one blow get revenge on the Philistines for my two eyes" (Judg. 16:28). Can we cry out for God to use us—at least once!—to glorify His name on the earth and to undo some of the damage Satan has done? Is this too much to ask? And is it conceivable that He could use us just twice, or even more?

Doesn't the very nature of God tell us something? Is there any image more powerful, more unrelenting, more intense, more overwhelming, more unwavering, more furious than the image of an immense consuming fire? That is the image of our God! He is an almighty, unquenchable blaze, an all-devouring fire (see Deut. 4:24; Heb. 12:29).

And this is the description of His Son:

His winnowing fork is in His hand, and He will clear His threshing floor, gathering His wheat into the barn and burning up the chaff with unquenchable fire. (Matt. 3:12)

But who can endure the day of His coming? Who can stand when He appears? For He will be like a refiner's fire or a launderer's soap. (Mal. 3:2)

> [On that day, the Lord says] So I will come near to you for judgment. I will be quick to testify against sorcerers, adulterers and perjurers, against those who defraud laborers of their wages, who oppress the widows and the fatherless, and deprive aliens of justice, but do not fear Me…. (Mal. 3:5)

The Lord will bring this testimony through us. Who else can it possibly come through?

But someone might say, "Does this really apply today? Weren't things different back in Bible days? After all, the people worshiped idols! Today people are more sophisticated. Surely modern, civilized man would never stoop to such depths. I'm just not convinced that today's gospel needs to be so confrontational."

Stop and think again. *Our society has left us no choice but to be confrontational.* In fact, love would no longer be love if it failed to rebuke this generation, and truth would no longer be truth if it failed to expose the lies.

Consider the curriculum being used in some of our schools. As of 1992, *first graders* were getting indoctrinated into homosexual and lesbian life styles. Little children (ages 3 to 8!) were learning to develop their reading skills with books like *Gloria Goes to Gay Pride*. One highly publicized story, *Daddy's Roommate*, contains these almost unbelievable lines:

> My Mommy and Daddy got a divorce last year. Now there's somebody new at Daddy's house. Daddy and his roommate Frank live together, work together, eat together, sleep together…. Mommy says Daddy and Frank are gay. At first I didn't know what that meant. So she explained it. Being

gay is just one more kind of love. And love is the best kind
of happiness....

## Homosexual activism is rampant!

Teacher's manuals urge the instructors *not* to encourage
"sexist" stereotypes (like little girls playing with dolls!)
and *fourth graders* are educated in the use of condoms, as
well as in concepts like oral and anal sex. But its gets lower
still! An AIDS tract published by the Division of AIDS Program Services, funded by the federal Centers for Disease
Control and the City of New York, and distributed in the
city's high schools, contains these words of wisdom for
teenagers, called: "The Teenager's Bill of Rights." (It is actually a "Bill of Death.")

> I have the right to think for myself.
> I have the right to decide whether to have sex and who to
>      have it with.
> I have the right to use protection when I have sex. [Later it
>      is explained: "Condoms can be sexy! They come in dif-
>      ferent colors, sizes, flavors, and styles to be more fun for
>      you and your partner...."]
> I have the right to buy and use condoms....

And remember, this perverse trash, which is not even fit
for a garbage can, is being distributed in the schools with
taxpayers' money. (That's right, with *your* money.) The
tract only gets worse from here. But it is too shameful to
be quoted any more.

I ask you: How can we *not* confront such filth? And
what kind of reaction can we expect from men and women
who have degraded themselves until they are willing to

*fight* for their depravity? The people of light must oppose and challenge the darkness—if we really still are light.

Please hear me! These are not the fanatical ramblings of someone who thinks the sky is falling. This is not religious hyperbole. No! America is in desperate trouble. Our nation is becoming totally undone. The whole fabric of our society is unraveling. *And darkness is enveloping the Church.*

How urgently true light is needed! How great is the need for God's people to proclaim Jesus and His standards! How critical this day is for our land! Who will arise and act? Who will stand and speak? God give us holy messengers in this hour!

*I cannot conceive it possible for anyone truly to receive Christ as Savior and yet not to receive him as Lord. A man who is really saved by grace does not need to be told that he is under solemn obligations to serve Christ. The new life within him tells him that. Instead of regarding it as a burden, he gladly surrenders himself—body, soul, and spirit—to the Lord who has redeemed him, reckoning this to be his reasonable service.*

Charles H. Spurgeon

*Christ as Savior is not divided. He that hath him not in all, shall have him in none at all of his offices in a saving manner.*

John Bunyan

*If we would have the LORD for our God, let us also take him for our King (Psa. 5:2). If we reject his laws, it is certain we reject his grace. If we refuse his yoke, we surely do not accept his mercy. If his sceptre is an offense to us, so is his plan of saving sinners by his blood.*

William Plumer

*Look once again to Jesus Christ in his death upon the cross...He carried our sin, our captivity and our suffering, and did not carry it in vain.* **He carried it away.** *He acted as the captain of us all. He broke through the ranks of our enemies. He has already won the battle. All we have to do is to follow him, to be victorious with him. Through him, in him we are saved. Our sin no longer has any power over us. Our prison door is open.... When he, the Son of God, sets us free, we are* **truly** *free.*

Karl Barth

# Chapter Three
# The Savior Is the Lord

*Jesus came to save us from our sins.* That is the heart of the gospel! It is true that He came to save us from hell, but hell is not our primary problem. Hell is only the consequence of the problem. *Sin* is the great problem of the human race. Jesus came to free us from our sins! That is what His name is all about.

> She will give birth to a son, and you are to give Him the name Jesus [short for "the Lord is salvation"], because *He will save His people from their sins.* (Matt. 1:21)

Anything less than that is not salvation. Anything less than that is not our Savior. That is why He came, bled, died, and rose from the dead: to free us from our sins! Yet somehow this truth is being missed in our day. In fact, at the heart of our contemporary, non-confrontational gospel is a failure to deal adequately with sin and a failure to present *Jesus the Lord* as the Savior from sin.

The modern message of salvation is soft on sin and lax on lordship. It de-emphasizes repentance by teaching: "Repentance is only a change of mind!" And it downplays conviction by saying: "Nowhere in the New Testament does it ever say we should be sorry for our sins!" (These are actual quotes from ministers whose sermons I have heard or whose books I have read.)

Of course, these ministers do not encourage believers to live in sin, nor do they tell the unsaved that sin is a good thing. But, by failing to teach the people clearly that following the Savior means forsaking their sins, they cut out the heart of the gospel. And they leave the door wide open for someone to think that they can be saved while actively serving another master (Satan!). What's more, these pastors, teachers and authors actually claim that their new emphasis is an *advance* in the revelation of grace—as if God's grace offered free tickets to Heaven to those who remain children of hell! That is not the gospel; that is grotesque. Nor is it grace; it is gross. The gospel of grace offers free salvation *from* our sins.

Is there any way to mistake the clear meaning of these Scriptures?

> The next day John saw Jesus coming toward him and said, "Look, the Lamb of God, who *takes away the sin of the world!*" (John 1:29)

> For we know that our old self was crucified with Him *so that the body of sin might be done away with, that we should no longer be slaves to sin.* (Rom. 6:6)

> He Himself bore our sins in His body on the tree, *so that we might die to sins and live for righteousness*; by His wounds you have been healed. (1 Pet. 2:24)

> ...To Him who loves us and *has freed us from our sins* by His blood, and has made us to be a kingdom and priests to

serve His God and Father—to Him be glory and power for
ever and ever! Amen. (Rev. 1:5-6)

Yet many today say, "God does not want us to preach
sin, He wants us to preach salvation." Amen! But salvation
from what? From hell? Yes! That is the message of John
3:16. But from sin too! Listen to First Corinthians 15:17:

And if Christ has not been raised, your faith is futile; you
are still in your sins.

And if He *is* raised from the dead?—thank God He is!—
then our faith is *not* futile and *we are no longer in our sins.*
If we are still in our sins—if sin is our life and our master—
then we are still enslaved. Slaves need to be redeemed. And
Jesus is the great Redeemer! He buys our freedom from
slavery to sin.

This confirms what Paul said earlier in this very same
epistle. After describing the sins of "the wicked" (sexual
immorality, idolatry, adultery, homosexuality, theft, greed,
drunkenness, slander and swindling), he writes, "And that
is what some of you *were*" (1 Cor. 6:11a).

Corinthian believers, you are no longer what you used
to be! Something radical happened. You have been born
from above. That is the work of redemption. Yet an influential theologian and internationally recognized preacher
claims this:

When Paul says "such were some of you," he was not referring merely to their pre-conversion past but to the way
"some" of them had been behaving since they had been
saved.

But that is not what Paul meant. Look at the whole passage:

> And that is what some of you were. But you were washed,
> you were sanctified, you were justified in the name of the
> Lord Jesus Christ and by the Spirit of our God. (1 Cor. 6:11)

In other words, radical transformation is the certain result
of being washed, sanctified and *justified*. That is the teaching of Paul.

> But thanks be to God that, though you used to be slaves to
> sin, you wholeheartedly obeyed the form of teaching to
> which you were entrusted. *You have been set free from sin
> and have become slaves to righteousness.* (Rom. 6:17-18)

> For He has *rescued* us from the dominion of darkness and
> *brought us into* the kingdom of the Son He loves, in whom
> we have redemption, the forgiveness of sins. (Col. 1:13-14)

That is salvation! The blood of Jesus both looses and
liberates. *Forgiveness of the debt of sin means freedom
from the domination of sin.* As Scottish evangelist James
Alexander Stewart emphasized many times: "Jesus does
not save us *in* our sins but *from* our sins." He explained
further:

> We are saved from a life of sin to a life of holiness.... Sal-
> vation is more than a passport to Heaven; it is deliverance
> from the dominion of sin in this life.

Unfortunately, many (and I mean many!) teach and
write in our day: "The sinner does not need to receive Jesus
as Lord in order to be saved. He only needs to receive Him
as Savior." But they have forgotten one essential thing: The
Savior is the Lord! He is not a schizophrenic! The Savior
whose return we "eagerly await" is *"the Lord* Jesus Christ"
(Phil. 3:20). It is not a debatable matter.

Look carefully at the New Testament writings. They never say, "Our Lord *or* Savior Jesus Christ," but "Our Lord *and* Savior Jesus Christ." He does not have a split personality! The New Testament does not say, "Our Savior and Lord, Jesus Christ," but "Our Lord and Savior, Jesus Christ." His lordship is always pre-eminent. In fact, if you take out an exhaustive concordance and do some counting, you will be shocked by what you find. *Jesus is called Lord more than 400 times just in the Book of Acts and the Epistles; He is called Savior just 15 times in the entire New Testament.* Our preaching emphasis is wrong! We have almost completely missed the point.

The Church and the world must hear clearly the proclamation of Jesus the Savior *as* Lord, and both sinners and saints must be called to submit to Him unconditionally. *The right proclamation will produce the right results.* (And it will certainly rock some boats!) Telling people that He is Lord (i.e., that He is divine), carries little weight unless it is coupled with the call to submit to His rule. Otherwise it is just empty theology. Empty theology has never saved anyone.

Although the modern gospel talks a lot about faith, it does not call sinners (by faith!) to surrender to the Lord. It tells them to merely believe that He *is* Lord (even the demons do that, and with trembling too), and that He is willing and able to forgive—even if the sinner continues in stubborn rebellion and defiant disobedience; even if he refuses to submit. *That is not the gospel.*

Let's set the record straight: The gospel (good news) is God's gracious offer to set us free from our sins and to give us a whole new life under the lordship of Jesus. How? By faith. It is a gift from God, plain and simple. We cannot earn it, buy it or deserve it. It is offered freely and without charge, as the Scriptures exhort and teach: "Turn away from your sins and turn back to God (that's repentance) and put your faith in the Lord Jesus to save you (see Paul's words in Acts 20:21), forgive you, cleanse you, transform you, deliver you and make you into a child of God, a priest of the Most High, and a slave of righteousness." *He* will do it all by His grace. That is God's glorious salvation!

But much contemporary preaching offers a partial salvation because it has forgotten most of the problem. Mankind rebelled against the Lord. That is what we call sin. Because of sin, the world became filled with sickness, violence, hatred, suffering and death. *The gospel deals effectively with the sin problem by calling sinners to give up their rebellion.*

Isaiah preached it:

Let the wicked forsake his way and the evil man his thoughts. Let him turn to the Lord, and He will have mercy on him, and to our God, for He will freely pardon. (Is. 55:7)

Ezekiel preached it:

...Repent! Turn away from all your offenses; then sin will not be your downfall. Rid yourselves of all the offenses you have committed, and get a new heart and a new spirit.... (Ezek. 18:30-31)

Peter preached it:

> Repent, then, and turn to God, so that your sins may be wiped out, that times of refreshing may come from the Lord. (Acts 3:19)

Paul preached it:

> ...I was not disobedient to the vision from heaven. First to those in Damascus, then to those in Jerusalem and in all Judea, and to the Gentiles also, I preached that they should repent and turn to God and prove their repentance by their deeds. (Acts 26:19-20)

The gospel calls people to choose life (grace) by renouncing death (sin). It says, "Seek Me and live" (Amos 5:4); but it also says, "Do not seek Bethel" (Amos 5:5). (In other words, don't seek idols any longer.) It says, "Abandon your sin and submit to the Lord by faith in the blood of the Lamb." That is the key to reconciliation: submitting once again to the rule of God by the power and grace of God.

Reconciliation means setting things right. It means removing the blemish of sin and breaking the bondage to sin. Anything less than that is defective. As Charles Spurgeon taught:

> Justification without sanctification would not be salvation at all. It would call the leper clean, and leave him to die of his disease; it would forgive the rebellion and allow the rebel to remain an enemy to the King. It would remove the consequences but overlook the cause, and this would leave an endless and hopeless task before us.

That is not the biblical gospel! *Jesus saves us from sin just as surely as He saves us from hell.*

Yet it is a largely non-biblical gospel that has flooded the pulpits, Christian bookstores, Bible schools and seminaries of our land. It has been quite a hit on TV too! The contemporary American version of the gospel deals strongly with the *penalty* and *punishment* of sin without fully addressing the *power* and *pollution* of sin. It says, "Be rescued from hell and wrath, but don't worry right now about being ransomed from your sins." It declares you free from the *condemnation* of sin without cleansing you from the *contamination* of sin. But it is sin's contamination that condemns, and sin's pollution that brings punishment.

God withdrew from the temple in Ezekiel's day because He would not, and could not, dwell together with idolatry, immorality and violence. The principle will never change: The Lamb will not be married to someone who remains wedded to his sins—in spite of what some modern teachers claim.

From a biblical viewpoint, nothing could be stranger than a "gospel" that doesn't tell sinners to turn from their sins. Listen to the message that the apostles preached:

> When God raised up His servant, He sent Him first to you to bless you *by turning each of you from your wicked ways.* (Acts 3:26)

> God exalted [Jesus] to His own right hand as Prince and Savior that He might give repentance and forgiveness of sins to Israel. (Acts 5:31; see also Luke 24:47! That's where the apostles got their message.)

"But," you say, "we must only tell them to believe. God will deal with their sins." God already *has* dealt with their sins: at Calvary. Now He says, "Believe that Jesus died to save you from your sins, and you can live the rest of your life for Me." Jesus died to set you free!

"But doesn't the Greek word for *repentance* only mean 'a change of mind'? Isn't God just telling us to change our minds about Jesus? Isn't this talk about 'being sorry for our sins' a carry-over from Old Testament legalistic bondage?" Absolutely not!

First, John the Baptist, Jesus, and all the apostles were first century Jews who spoke Aramaic (and probably Hebrew), and the fundamental Aramaic and Hebrew word for *repent* means "turn around, turn back, do an about-face." (The other Hebrew word used for *repent* means "feel sorrow, grief and regret; have second thoughts, change your mind.") Second, the New Testament makes it perfectly clear that the *proof* of repentance is seen in one's actions (read Luke 3:7-14 and Acts 26:20). Third, the best scholars of New Testament Greek understand the Greek words *metanoeo* (repent) and *metanoia* (repentance) to mean more than just a change of mind.

The authoritative *Theological Dictionary of the New Testament* states:

> ...*metanoeo* and *metanoia* are the forms in which the NT gives new expression to the ancient concept of religious and moral conversion.... [The repentance preaching of Jesus] demands radical conversion, a transformation of nature, a definitive turning from evil, a resolute turning to God in total obedience (Mk. 1:15; Mt. 4:17; 18:3).

A.T. Robertson, one of the greatest Greek scholars of the century, taught that the New Testament preaching of repentance said:

> Change your mind and life. Turn right about and do it now.

The widely acclaimed *New International Dictionary of New Testament Theology* says:

> The predominantly intellectual understanding of *metanoia* as change of mind plays very little part in the NT. Rather the decision by the whole man to turn around is stressed. It is clear that we are concerned neither with a purely outward turning nor with a merely intellectual change of ideas.

Just think of how silly it would be if "repent" only meant "change your mind." The words of Jesus would then become preposterous:

> Woe to you, Korazin! Woe to you, Bethsaida! If the miracles that were performed in you had been performed in Tyre and Sidon, they would have *changed their mind* [?!] long ago *in sackcloth and ashes* (Matt. 11:21)?

No! They would have "repented long ago in sackcloth and ashes."

John's baptism would have become nonsense:

> ...a baptism of *changing of mind* [?!] for the *forgiveness of sins* (Luke 3:3)?

No! It was a baptism of "repentance" for forgiveness of sins.

If repentance is only a change of mind, with no conviction involved, then why did Paul tell the Corinthians: "*Godly sorrow* brings repentance that leads to salvation and leaves no regret..." (2 Cor. 7:10)?

Is it too much to think that the sinner should feel sorry that he has sinned against God Almighty? Was this primarily an Old Testament phenomenon? (I've heard that taught too!) Is it unreasonable to believe that when the transgressor realizes it was his own sin that nailed the Savior to the cross, he might be cut to the heart? Did James (in the New Testament, no less) know what he was doing when he called on sinners to "grieve, mourn and wail" (James 4:9)? Or was Jesus misinformed when *He* defined repentance? (That's right! *Jesus* offered a definition of repentance too.)

Look carefully at Luke 15, where the Lord gave a threefold parable, speaking of the lost sheep, the lost coin and the lost (prodigal) son. After speaking of the shepherd's joy when he finds his lost sheep, Jesus said:

> I tell you that in the same way there will be more rejoicing in heaven over one sinner who repents than over ninety-nine righteous persons who do not need to repent. (Luke 15:7)

Likewise, after speaking of the joy of the woman who found her lost coin, Jesus said:

> In the same way, I tell you, there is rejoicing in the presence of the angels of God over one sinner who repents. (Luke 15:10)

Then, speaking of the prodigal son, the Lord explained exactly what this "repentance" is all about: The young man, languishing in his foolish independence from his father, comes to his senses. He humbles himself, regrets what he has done, and resolves to return to his father, confess his sin, and plead for mercy (Luke 15:14-21). *That is the Lord's own description of a sinner repenting.* And the

prodigal's father, just like our Father, completely wel-
comed him back. The rejoicing was, and is, great!

Not all sinners will be deeply convicted of sin when they
get saved. But if we preach the right message with the
anointing of God, it will be the rule rather than the exception.

Of course, we do not tell the unsaved: "Feel bad, become good, reform your ways and then believe." Absolutely not! If the Holy Spirit is dealing with them, we tell them,
"Right now, in your heart, cry out to God to save you from
your sins by the blood of Jesus. Right now, with your
mouth, ask Him to deliver you from the snare of the devil
and to make you His own. Give up your sinful self-will and
turn back to God. Die to your own will and your own life.
Jesus will deliver you and make you whole! Put your faith
in Him."

How different this is from some of the empty invitations
I have heard on "Christian" television or listened to on
audio cassette: "If you believe in my prayers [this famous
evangelist didn't even mention Jesus], raise your hand and
I'll pray for your salvation"; or, "Just say, 'Jesus, You're
my Lamb. I trust You.' " (There wasn't even a hint that sin
should be forsaken!) Does that even resemble the biblical
message?

Any gospel that does not preach salvation from hell
without also preaching salvation from sin is a defective,
deficient and, at times, even damnable gospel. In fact, if
Jesus does not save us from our sins, if He does not deliver
us from the domination of the devil, if He does not redeem

us from slavery and bondage, then He is not the Savior we need and He is not even worthy of the name Jesus.

God's purpose was to get a holy Bride for His Son. It was for that Bride that Jesus came into this filthy world, and it is through faith in Him that we become part of that Bride. (Remember, Heaven will not be populated with slaves of Satan, but with servants of the Son.) Let your spirit drink in the testimony of God's Word. *The main reason we preach a confrontational message is so there will be a glorious Bride for the Son.*

Why did God make Him who had no sin to be a sin offering for us?

So that in Him we might become the righteousness of God. (2 Cor. 5:21b)

Why did God condemn sin in sinful man?

In order that the righteous requirements of the law might be fully met in us, who do not live according to the sinful nature but according to the Spirit. (Rom. 8:4)

Why did the Messiah love the Church and give Himself up for her?

To make her holy, cleansing her by the washing with water through the word, and to present her to Himself as a radiant church, without stain or wrinkle or any other blemish, but holy and blameless. (Eph. 5:26-27)

Why did God choose us in Jesus before the creation of the world?

[So we might] be holy and blameless in His sight.... (Eph. 1:4b)

...from the beginning God chose you to be saved through the sanctifying work of the Spirit and through belief in the truth. (2 Thess. 2:13)

[He] has saved us and called us to a holy life—not because of anything we have done but because of His own purpose and grace. (2 Tim. 1:9a)

As believers, if we confess and turn from our sins (see Prov. 28:13), then "the blood of Jesus, His Son, purifies us from all sin" (1 John 1:7).

Thank God for *cleansing* from sin! Faith in Jesus sets us *free*.

\* \* \* \*

About a hundred years ago, William Booth, the passionate soul winner and founder of the Salvation Army, uttered these prophetic words:

The chief danger of the twentieth century will be:
Religion without the Holy Ghost,
Christianity without Christ,
Forgiveness without repentance,
Salvation without regeneration,
Heaven without hell.

What will the twenty-first century hold?

*He that thinks to please men goes about an endless and needless work. A wise physician seeks to cure, not please, his patient. (Written on the duties of ministers regarding preaching the Word.)*

William Gurnall

*Ministers are not cooks, but physicians and therefore should not study to delight the palate, but to recover the patient.*

Jean Daille

*Secure sinners must hear the thundering of Mount Sinai before we bring them to Mount Zion. Every minister should be a Boanerges, a son of thunder, as well as Barnabas, a son of consolation.*

George Whitefield

*I would rather have a moderately small meeting of earnest Christians than to have it packed with thousands of careless people.*

D. L. Moody

*Where all approve, few profit.*

John Wesley

*Speaking for a national morality movement, an evangelical leader recently remarked: "The United States has turned away from God. It mocks God. It worships a twentieth century Baal...incarnated in sensuality, material goods, and immorality of every kind"...Yet only a few years ago we were told that a new evangelical awakening had dawned in America; this very decade, it was said, is the decade of the evangelicals. (Written in 1985.)*

Carl F. H. Henry

# Chapter Four

# Connoisseur Christians and a Gourmet Gospel

Believers today are a hard bunch to please, but it's not because we're so spiritual. It's because we're so spoiled! If the weekly serving of the Scriptures doesn't suit our tastes, we'll go somewhere else where the menu is more to our liking. We're so pampered and picky that the moment the Spirit penetrates our plump, plush world we close our ears, harden our hearts, and cry, "Condemnation! That's a negative message! It's too hard, too strong, too blunt! After all, we go to church to get pumped up, not pierced through. We come to be satisfied, not to squirm!"

Of course, nowadays, if we're not happy with our local preachers, we don't even need to change churches. That requires too much effort. No, the solution is as close as the TV remote control! With so much gospel entertainment on the air waves, we're bound to find some television "pastor" who will amuse us with his mannerisms and amaze us with his miracles. Best of all, if we don't like what *they* have to say, all we do is flip the switch. We don't even have to get out of our easy chair!

If the prosperity message doesn't hit the spot today, we can hear some tasty teaching on "How to Accept Yourself." If some end-time prophecy nuggets don't satisfy, there's bound to be a delectable morsel or two in the repeat broadcast of the "Learning to Live with Food Addiction" seminar. If none of that is appetizing, there are some "meaty" verses in the Word itself, like John 10:10 (which is something about Jesus coming into the world so we could be super-blessed). Maybe we can discover a new spiritual key to success!

It's sad to say, but today's believers would have had a hard time sitting through some of Jeremiah's sermons, let alone relating to a fanatic-type like John the locust eater. I can almost hear our modern-day gourmet gang analyzing these anointed servants of God. It might have sounded something like this...

**JEREMIAH**: Too negative! All he seems to talk about is *judgment*. I come to the Temple to get some joy in my life. This guy's an absolute joy-stealer! In fact, I think he's got some real hang-ups. All this weeping! He obviously suffers from rejection—and I'll bet he's projecting *his* rejection onto us! I hope he gets some inner healing soon. Until then, I'm staying away from this character.

In the meantime, I've got some advice for him: Lighten up, Jeremiah. It wouldn't hurt you to smile a little. This gloom and doom stuff has gotten the better of you. Things will turn around for the better soon. They *always* do!

**JOEL**: Too emotional! What's with this call for wailing and mourning? How dare he tell me how to touch God! He even has the audacity to *order* me to rend my heart and not my garment. Who told *him* that my heart isn't broken? Who told *him* that tearing my clothes isn't meaningful? It was meaningful for Joel's father and my father! Where is it written that if I don't scream I'm not sincere? These Pentecostals. They're always mistaking noise for nearness. They all think the sky's about to fall!

I'll tell you, this Joel is a dreamer. He's *carried away* with his own emotions. He says that one day the Spirit will fall on *everybody* and then *all flesh* will prophesy. Right! I'll bet they'll speak a new language too! Sorry Joel, but this emotional stuff is not for me.

**EZEKIEL**: Too weird! The guy is simply out of touch. Really, he's got some deep emotional problems. He won't talk; he digs through the city wall (carrying a suitcase at the same time!); he sighs when he eats; he cuts off his hair and then burns it, throws it into the wind, and tries to hack it up with a knife—*while it's flying through the air.* What a sight! The poor guy lies on one side for 390 days and his other side for 40 more days and, get this, he says *God* told him to do it all! Show me where Moses ever did such a thing! But it gets worse. He wants us to believe that he's a prophet, a divine spokesman, and he claims that *Jerusalem*, the city of the Lord, is going to fall to the Babylonians! I can sum up this deluded chump in one word: *dysfunctional.*

**HOSEA**: Too carnal! He obviously has a problem with women. Just think: He marries a prostitute and he frequents the slave markets. What kind of example is this for the young people? What's become of the ministry today? I remember the time when people like him would be put out! Soon he'll probably tell us that his wife is a prophetess too.

The poor guy is obviously under a spirit of deception. He thinks *God* is telling him to do what he actually wants to do. He also makes everything into a divinely ordained event: Each time he touches his wife, each time they have a baby, each time they name a new child, it's some kind of prophetic act. Why can't he be like everyone else? To listen to him speak, you'd think he was actually producing Scripture. It's clear: He's deceived!

**ISAIAH**: Too lofty! He spends too much time with the upper crust of society. I hear he even plays golf with the king! I want a preacher, not an aristocrat. Oh sure, I'll admit that he's a good speaker; he really knows how to use alliteration, and he's a gifted poet too. But I'm a meat and potatoes type of guy. Give it to me simple and straight. All this "mounting up on wings like eagles" stuff leaves me cold. I've learned to distinguish between the mind and the heart. With Isaiah, it's all mind, no heart. His ministry will never stand the test of time.

**JOHN THE BAPTIST**: Too harsh! I hate to say it, but this guy arrived late on the scene and his parents, well, let's just say that they never put him in his place. They were so happy to have a kid of their own that they catered to his every whim and fancy. That's why he always thinks *he's* right and the whole world is wrong. That's why he's so sure that *he's* the chosen messenger (something about being the forerunner of the Lord). It's typical of the "only child syndrome": They think everything revolves around them!

You know, I don't even feel sorry for John, even though he's in prison. After all, he asked for it. Who told him to meddle in the king's personal affairs? He would have been better off just sticking to his "Behold the Lamb of God" sermon. *That* was good preaching! Mark my words: Twenty years from now, when he's married and has a grown family of his own, he'll be a lot more mellow. Some things just take time.

**JOHN THE APOSTLE**: Too spiritual! All he ever talks about is God and love. "God is love and love is God. God loves you so you love God." If you've heard him once, you've heard him a thousand times. He may be sincere, but his message is too simple, not to mention the fact that it's impractical. He needs to come down to earth. John, talk to us about everyday things like sports, jobs and politics. Be concrete. All this "light and darkness" stuff doesn't touch my life. And, John, we're not babies! Enough with this "don't hate your brother" stuff. Give us a little credit, huh? Give us some *meat*.

**PAUL**: Too confusing! First he says judge everything, then he says judge nothing, then he says judge yourself, but he won't judge *himself*! First he tells us that the doers of the law will be justified, then he says that *no one* will be justified by the law. You know what? I think the guy likes to hear himself talk! I bet he doesn't understand what he's saying either! (He once preached so long a guy fell asleep and almost killed himself. Of course, they made Paul out to be a hero in that episode too!)

This "meek and timid" Paul is always telling us how humble he is, but only after calling himself the most anointed apostle of them all. Then he's got this persecution complex: Everywhere he goes he seems to get into trouble. (Of course, according to *his* version of the story, he never does anything to deserve it!) If I had the time, I would check into this guy's background. Chances are he comes from a co-dependent family.

**JESUS**: Too radical! He makes totally unrealistic demands. He tells people that if they want to be His disciples, they have to leave *everything*, deny themselves, and take up their cross daily. He's obviously not a family man. He orders people to *hate* their parents, and tells them that if they don't love *Him* more than *them*, they're not worthy of Him. It's clear He doesn't have a shepherd's heart; I hear He once called a needy Canaanite woman a dog, and He was totally insensitive to a son grieving for his dad who had just died. He said, "Let someone else bury your father. You come after Me!"

To judge by His followers, He's not very deep either. Only the fishermen, tax collectors, political activists and prostitutes seem to be impressed by Him. The religious leaders know better! He's so undignified too: He *spits* when He heals people, He talks out loud to demons, and actually *touches* lepers and corpses. Worst of all, He has this death fixation. He keeps talking about being crucified in Jerusalem. If He's not careful, He's going to find Himself in a heap of trouble pretty soon.

Jesus, take it from me. If You get some good seminary training under Your belt, tone down Your message, and quit offending Your spiritual elders, You'll live a lot longer. Think of how many more people You could help if You could avoid a premature death.

And think of all the people *we* could help...if we could only have it our way.

*The most of God's people are contented to be saved from the hell that is without. They are not so anxious to be saved from the hell that is within.*

Robert Murray M'Cheyne

*I set myself on fire, and the people come to see me burn. (When asked how he drew the crowds.)*

John Wesley

*It was evident that they somehow resented my plain dealing, and that my searching sermons astonished, and even offended, very many of them. However, as the work went forward, this state of things changed greatly; and after a few weeks they would listen to searching preaching, and came to appreciate it.*

Charles G. Finney

*Speak every time, my dear brother, as if it were your last; weep out, if possible, every argument; and compel them to cry, "Behold, how He loves us."*

George Whitefield

*We need a trumpet voice again to tell sluggish believers that God requires holiness of His people. **There is a famine of true holiness preaching.***

Leonard Ravenhill

*You are all guilt; He is a fountain to wash you. You are all naked; He has a wedding garment to cover you. You are dead; He is the life. You are all wounds and bruises; He is the Balm of Gilead.*

M'Cheyne

# Chapter Five

# Separating the Wheat From the Chaff

There is no doubt that there are presently millions of pampered believers in America. Their taste for quality preaching is quite poor. But it is equally true that there is plenty of quite poor preaching! In fact, *most* preaching today is characterized by lack of anointing, lack of fire, and lack of convicting power.

There is a two-fold problem: Connoisseur Christians don't have much good preaching to pick from, and when it *is* there, they don't recognize it! They're like children who love their sweets but hate their salads, or like the on-campus college students who think they can live on candy bars and Coke. Pampered pew sitters like to eat, but what they like to eat isn't healthy!

There *is* every reason for believers today to be hungry for more meat from the Word. The problem is we have developed an appetite for junk, not for nourishment; for fluff, not for food. Yes, there is reason for many believers to say, "But my pastor *is* too negative" (or, too emotional, too boring, too long-winded, too confusing, too dull, etc., etc.). The problem is, using the same criteria, we would not have found the biblical prophets and apostles to our liking either!

John Wesley encountered the same phenomenon in his day. People had problems with his preaching because he didn't "conform to what he disparagingly referred to as 'a luscious way of talking.' This was what passed for a gospel message in some circles, and Wesley repudiated it" (A. Skevington Wood). What did he mean by a "luscious way of talking"? He was apparently referring to a "luscious preaching of the gospel made up all of promises, and these wholly unconditional" (John Worthington).

Wesley lamented that once people got used to this all-fluff gospel message, they lost their taste for solid food. His sharp criticism of shallow preaching sounds as if it had been written yesterday:

Why, this is the very thing I assert: that the "gospel preachers" so called corrupt their hearers; they vitiate their taste, so that they cannot relish sound doctrine; and spoil their appetite, so that they cannot turn it into nourishment; they, as it were, feed them with sweetmeats, till the genuine wine of the kingdom seems quite insipid to them. They give them cordial upon cordial [i.e., alcoholic drink upon drink], which make them all life and spirit for the present; but meantime their appetite is destroyed, so that they can neither retain nor digest the pure milk of the Word. Hence it is that (according to the constant observation I have made in all parts both of England and Ireland) preachers of this kind (though quite the contrary appears at first), spread death not life, among their hearers. As soon as the flow of spirits [i.e., alcoholic beverages] goes off, they are without life, without power, without any strength or vigour of soul; and it is extremely difficult to recover them, because they still cry out, "Cordials, cordials!" of which they have had too much already, and have no taste for the food convenient for them. Nay, they have an utter aversion to it, and that confirmed by principle, having been taught to call it husks, if not poison.

What an amazing quote! People who get pumped up by a lightweight gospel message *seem* to be filled with spiritual life and energy, but just try to call them to sacrifice or to biblical standards of holiness and they cry out, "That's not the Spirit of God!" These same people who seem to have so much vitality can't even make it through the day without getting "pumped up" again with the same "positive" message. They have almost no spiritual reserve! Why? They are hooked on soulish teaching that produces little more than an emotional lift.

Such preaching can be downright damaging. In fact, Wesley claimed that preaching that emphasized salvation by faith *without* a strong emphasis on holiness was actually...

the most useless, if not the most mischievous.... I see more and more that this naturally tends to drive holiness out of the world.

What we need today is more Spirit-filled, Jesus-exalting, Bible-based, life-changing preaching and teaching of the holy Word of a holy God. What we need today is more wheat, not chaff. How can we tell the difference? Here are some questions to ask:

**Does this preaching glorify Jesus?** The central theme of the Word is not faith, love, prayer, holiness, repentance, evangelism, relationship, covenant, the Church, Israel, spiritual gifts, or even the Word itself. The central theme of the Word is Jesus, the Messiah, Savior, and Lord—to the glory of God the Father. That must be our theme too! It must make our hearts sing and inspire our preaching.

John the Baptist understood this truth emphatically. The whole reason he came baptizing with water "was that [Jesus] might be revealed to Israel" (John 1:31). The goal of his preaching—and of his whole life—was that Jesus might become greater and he might become less (John 3:30). That's why the Lord called John the greatest prophet who ever lived.

How do today's preachers measure up? How many can say, "The whole reason I minister is so Jesus may be revealed"? How many are great in *God's* eyes? How many know the first thing about "the unsearchable riches of Christ" (Eph. 3:8)?

And those of us with a strong burden for the purity of the Body must remember something essential: Jesus, not sin, must be our emphasis! *Preachers who major on sin and minor on Jesus are like a bridegroom who takes his eyes off his precious bride as she walks down the aisle and focuses instead on a fly on her gown.* We need to stay centered on our Savior and Lord!

**Does this preaching bring me closer to the Lord? Does it cause me to press in to God through prayer and the Word? Does it strengthen my relationship with Him?**

Outside of the Vine, we have no life (John 15:1-7). He is the living Word (John 1:1,14); the bread of life (John 6:35); the way, the truth and the life (John 14:6); and the resurrection and the life (John 11:24-25). We must feed on Him to live. Sound preaching of the Word will point us directly to the Source of life and cause us to become more dependent on Him. Also, since *God* is at the very center of the Word, real biblical teaching and preaching will put *Him* in the very center of *us*.

Genuine ministry of the Word will cause us to hunger for more of God, not for more things. It will heighten our desire to please Him rather than to please ourselves.

**Does this preaching expose sin? Does it bring conviction? Does it provide an antidote to sin?** Light makes everything visible, and God's Word is a light (Ps. 119:105). It shines on both sinner and saint! (Read the following chapter for the details.) As James wrote, the Word is like a mirror. When we look into it, we see what we are really like. Faithful preaching of the Word will show us our true condition (like it or not) and show us the way out. The believer who looks intently into this "perfect law that gives freedom" and *acts on what he sees* "will be blessed in what he does" (James 1:25).

Of course, many of us don't even want to look into the mirror. We are like overweight people who avoid getting on the scales. But the facts are the facts. *Look in the mirror.* If the message hits a sore spot, rather than denying that it's from God, we must keep looking into that word from Heaven, believing that the God who sent it designed it for life, not death, for freedom and not bondage. And let the Holy Spirit, the One who anoints the preaching of the Word, do His convicting work on us. He knows what He is doing! If you have the privilege of hearing truly Spirit-anointed preaching, don't resist the disciplining hand of the Lord and grieve away this golden opportunity.

**Does this preaching correct and rebuke as well as encourage and instruct? Does it tell the truth? Is it "according to the Scriptures"?** Let these verses speak for themselves, then evaluate what you are hearing by these standards that God has set:

> Better is open *rebuke* than hidden love. *Wounds* from a friend can be trusted, but an enemy multiplies kisses. (Prov. 27:5-6)

> He who *rebukes* a man will in the end gain more favor than he who has a flattering tongue. (Prov. 28:23)

> Let a righteous man *strike* me—it is a kindness; let him *rebuke* me—it is oil on my head. My head will not refuse it. (Ps. 141:5)

> All Scripture is God-breathed and is useful for *teaching, rebuking, correcting* and *training* in righteousness, so that the man of God may be thoroughly equipped for every good work. (2 Tim. 3:16-17)

If you are getting only "taught" from the pulpit, without ever getting rebuked, corrected or trained (of course, it should be with gentleness out of a loving heart, not with harshness out of a domineering spirit), then you are not getting "thoroughly equipped for every good work." Your diet is deficient! To this end, Paul exhorted Timothy in the strongest possible terms:

> In the presence of God and of Christ Jesus, who will judge
> the living and the dead, and in view of His appearing and
> His kingdom, I give you this charge: Preach the Word; be
> prepared in season and out of season; *correct, rebuke* and
> *encourage*—with great patience and careful instruction.
> (2 Tim. 4:1-2)

May every minister of the gospel heed Paul's urgent
charge! *Flattery is of the devil.* Young Elihu had it right:

> I will show partiality to no one, nor will I flatter any man;
> for if I were skilled in flattery, my Maker would soon take
> me away. (Job 32:21-22)

Pastors, speak the truth in love. Follow the pattern of
the Son of God in Revelation 2 and 3. He did not mislead
the churches. He did not stroke the sinful. He was painfully
honest, commending and criticizing each congregation as
needed, always leaving them with hope if they would
respond. He is the great Shepherd of the sheep. Shouldn't
the undershepherds follow His lead?

> Those whom I love [said Jesus] I *rebuke* and *discipline*. So
> be earnest, and repent. (Rev. 3:19)

**Does this preaching ever make the flesh uncomfort-
able? Does it help move me to action?** A contemporary
Christian singer has written, "The cross is a radical thing."
Dying is not fun for the flesh. Denying yourself is not pleasant
for the natural man. Yet it is the only way to life! In fact, denying ourselves and taking up the cross are only the first steps
to actively following Jesus. That means action!

> Then He said to them all: "If anyone would come after Me,
> he must deny himself and take up his cross daily [notice that
> this is an everyday thing] and *follow Me*." (Luke 9:23)

Good preaching will keep us moving!

The Spirit is not stationary. Neither is He stuck. With a world ravaged by darkness and deceit, starvation and sickness, idolatry and immorality, hatred and homosexuality, racism and rebellion, how can we *not* do something? How is it possible that a God who loves this ugly, fallen world will not challenge us to service and sacrifice through His Word? With so many needs within the Body, how can the Head be silent? Listen carefully for the prodding of the Lord, and do not resist Him, whatever He says!

**Does this preaching carry conviction? Is it part of the minister's own experience in God? Or is it a recycled version of someone else's revelation?** Today we have a plague of parroting preachers. They are guilty of following in the footsteps of the false prophets of Jeremiah 23:30-31:

> "Therefore," declares the Lord, "I am against the prophets who steal from one another words supposedly from Me. Yes," declares the Lord, "I am against the prophets who wag their own tongues and yet declare, 'The Lord declares.'"

It is one thing to embrace another minister's message when it bears witness with your own and resonates deep within. It is another thing to be what has been called a "pulpit parrot." This kind of preaching goes only skin deep. It does not lastingly move the heart because the preacher can impact others only to the extent that God has impacted him. How shallow and unpenetrating so many messages are in our day! They come from shallow hearts.

We could learn a lesson here from the Puritans. They believed: "There is not a sermon which is heard, but it sets us nearer heaven or hell" (John Preston). Therefore, they preached *from* the heart as well as from the head, and *to* the heart as well as to the head. They aimed for depth!

> I preached what I felt, what I smartingly did feel.... Indeed I have been as one sent unto them from the dead. I went myself in chains to preach to them in chains; and carried that fire in my own conscience that I persuaded them to beware of (John Bunyan).

> I preached, as never sure to preach again,
> And as a dying man to dying men (Richard Baxter).

**Does this preaching present the grace of God? Does it give me hope? Does it produce faith to believe and to receive?** Paul spoke of "the incomparable riches of [God's] grace, expressed in His kindness to us in Christ Jesus" (Eph. 2:7). This is what God will display in the coming ages! Spirit-led preachers should boast even now in this glorious, life-changing truth. *Our God is the Author of grace.* So in Him we always have hope. That's why the prophet Amos could thunder with divine rebukes for eight painful chapters, only to end with hope in chapter 9. For the upright, light dawns in the darkness (Ps. 112:4).

Right teaching of the Word will inevitably build our faith: When we hear the promises of our all-faithful, never-failing Father, and when we understand that He grants us faith through His Word, what else can we do but believe? How can we not receive? If Jesus our great High Priest is being presented in the preaching, how can we not have hope?

**Does this preaching emphasize the love of God?** For the committed believer, there is nothing more encouraging, more uplifting, more inspiring than solid, biblical preaching of the love of God. For us, God's dearly loved children, what could be more wonderful than a message about our Father's love? What more could we ever want to hear? *There can never be too much preaching about the goodness of the Lord*—as long as we don't leave out the rest of the message! (See Romans 11:22; we must consider His goodness as well as His severity.)

The mercy and loving kindness of God—expressed to us through the sacrifice of His Son—must be steadily declared from the pulpit. As David Wilkerson recently wrote:

> The daily life of a majority of Christians...is not one of walking and believing in God's love. Instead, they live under a cloud of guilt, fear, condemnation. They have never really been free—they have never rested in God's love for them.

Of course, many believers are not at rest because their lives are so clogged with sin and disobedience. But, where there has been true repentance and godly sorrow (often as the result of a fresh revelation of the Father's love!) then, Wilkerson says, it's "time to move on to the banquet hall of love—to the feast!" We will feast forever on the riches of God's infinite love.

**Does this preaching motivate me to holy living? Does it produce lasting fruit (without the need for almost constant reaffirmation and refilling)? Does it lead to victorious living?** The believers in Rome "wholeheartedly obeyed the form of teaching to which [they] were entrusted" (Rom. 6:17). As a result, they were set free from sin and became slaves to righteousness (Rom. 6:18). We need more of that "form of teaching" today!

Paul's converts endured. Think of the Thessalonians whom Paul had to leave shortly after their conversion. He could write about their "work produced by faith," their "labor prompted by love," and their "endurance inspired by hope in our Lord Jesus Christ" (1 Thess. 1:3; see 2 Thess. 1:4 too). This is the result of solid spiritual food: well-nourished believers, overcoming the enemy, casting down temptation, refusing to quit, bearing fruit for God.

All that stands in stark contrast to so much of what we hear on radio and television, read in Christian books and magazines, and experience in our churches. So many of the messages we hear cause us to relax and become complacent. *They insulate us from the dealings of God.* Other teachings lead us to put ourselves first, to exalt self, or to bring glory and attention to man (like the famous television preacher who rallied his audience to proclaim out loud, "I'm a god! I'm a god!"). How much more "un-Christian" can we get?

The messages of so many modern "ministers" produce independence and arrogance instead of dependence and brokenness. In fact, their teaching is *calculated* to bring forth such rotten fruit, all in the name of "asserting our rights in Christ" and "coming into our inheritance." (In other words, "I get what I want when I want it!") But what about His rights over us? What about the fact that *He* has purchased *us* and that *we* are *His* inheritance?

And, in all fairness, let's not forget the extreme version of the old-time holiness message: "hard preaching" that instead of condemning sin actually condemns the saints, thereby destroying hope and bringing about death instead of life. (Those of you who say "Amen" to books like the one you are now reading have to be careful not to fall into this trap!) It is not biblical either.

Where then do you go? What should you do if you're being soothed into spiritual stupor and flattered into faithless flab? What if you're always being caressed and never challenged, only coddled and never convicted, constantly comforted and never confronted?

First, search your own heart. Make sure that you really want to hear "the whole counsel of God." Maybe the reason you're not hearing something new is because you have persistently refused to obey something old!

Second, get rid of all "extra-curricular" trash. There is a lot of teaching on Christian radio and television, as well as in the bookstores, that is hardly worthy of our time. Be discerning, not deceived.

Third, pray for your pastors and leaders, especially if you see that something is really wrong. If you can, share your heart with them. Don't condemn them, don't gossip about them, and don't be divisive or rebellious. But if things don't improve, if you continue to be *dangerously* malnourished and underfed, if there is *no* openness to spiritual change or interaction, then you might have to go somewhere else (really, this isn't the end of the world!) where you can effectively serve, submit and be fed.

Most important of all, *get into the Word for yourself.* Read it, meditate on it, memorize it, recite it, repeat it, devour it, obey it, believe it. No preacher can ever substitute for that.

And remember: Any message that breeds complacency is not of God. Any message that comforts the unconvicted is not of God. Any message that downplays the ugliness of sin is not of God. (You need to beware of pastors and evangelists who make light of sin!) Any message that bypasses the cross—the Savior's cross or our own—is not of God. Any message that robs the saints of their hope is not of God.

So if your heart is pure before the Lord, let no one condemn you! If it's not, let no one put you to sleep. You may never be able to awake.

*I have read of some barbarous nations who, when the sun shines hot upon them, shoot up their arrows against it—so do wicked men the light and heat of godliness.*

Jeremiah Burroughs

*Praise be to God, now we can practice sodomy!* (Spoken by a newly elected Florence official, immediately after the hanging of Savonarola, the prophetic priest, 1498.)

*Scripture is the Word of God, and it judges man thoroughly. It lays bare the very roots of his nature—it opens up the foundations of his moral being.*

C. H. Mackintosh

*As we try God's Word, so God's Word tries us; and happy [are we] if, when we are tried, we come forth as gold.*

William Jay

*It does not say, make your light shine. If it is really a light it will shine in spite of you—only don't hide it under a bushel. Let it shine. Confess Christ everywhere.*

D. L. Moody

# Chapter Six

# The Light Makes Everything Visible

John was the apostle of love, and his gospel was the gospel of love. It was John who recorded the immortal words: "For God so loved the world that He gave His one and only Son..." (John 3:16). It was John who informed us that "God did not send His Son into the world to condemn the world, but to save the world through Him" (John 3:17). It was John who presented to us a totally confrontational Jesus. The Jesus of John's Gospel was no longer a Babe in Bethlehem!

But some teachers have pointed out that John never uses the word *repent* in his Gospel. (Leonard Ravenhill reminds us that the word *hell* is never used in John's Gospel either. Does that mean we stop believing in hell?) The argument runs like this: "You can be saved without repenting. John says so himself. Jesus says so Himself. Just read the fourth Gospel!" Well, let's read it!

What can we learn from John 3:16-21, one of the most famous passages in the Bible? God did not send His Son into the world to condemn the world, He sent Him to confront it. He did not send Jesus to *expel* sinners, He sent Him to *expose* them. *Love is confrontational.* Look closely at these words:

> This is the verdict: Light has come into the world, but men loved darkness instead of light because their deeds were evil. Everyone who does evil hates the light, and will not come into the light for fear that his deeds will be exposed. (John 3:19-20)

> For it is light that makes everything visible.... (Eph. 5:14)

Throughout John's Gospel, Jesus brings the hidden things to light and exposes the evil deeds of the world. He reveals the hypocrisy of the religious elite; He uncovers the unseen attitudes of men's hearts; He calls on people to come out of the darkness. But coming out means coming clean!

Consider the Lord's ministry to the Samaritan woman. He invited her to partake of His living water, "a spring of water welling up to eternal life" (John 4:14). Then He got down to business: "Go, call your husband and come back" (John 4:16). Suddenly the atmosphere changed. Within a few seconds her sinful life was exposed, and she knew she had met a prophet.

> Come, see a man who told me everything I ever did. Could this be the Christ [Messiah]? (John 4:29)

Now ask yourself a question: Why didn't Jesus call this stranger by name? That certainly would have surprised her. Or why didn't He whisper her street address, or remind her of what she dreamed about the previous night? That would have gotten her attention. No. He confronted her in her sin: "The fact is, you have had five husbands, and the man you now have is not your husband..." (John 4:18). Shades of Paul with Felix and John the Baptist with Herod! Do you see a pattern developing?

The gracious offer of eternal life stands firm. It is absolutely free. But you must abandon your sin to enjoy it! "No one can serve two masters" (Matt. 6:24a). Jesus demands allegiance. He will shower His grace on us, but we must follow Him—and that means walking in the light.

> You are all sons of the light and sons of the day. We do not belong to the night or to the darkness. (1 Thess. 5:5)

> So let us put aside the deeds of darkness and put on the armor of light. (Rom. 13:12b)

*That* is the message of John. If you want to know the Son, you must come out of the darkness into His light. No one who hates the light can enter God's Kingdom!

Now turn to John 8:1-11, the account of the woman caught in adultery. Somehow this passage has been used to lightly excuse sin. After all, the woman was caught in the act and Jesus let her off. But did He simply "let her off"? No, He didn't. He extended to her complete pardon, going far beyond the bounds of the law. He did not condemn her. *Neither did He condone her.* "Go now and leave your life of sin" (John 8:11).

The same One who forgives our sins commands us to forsake our sins. Reconciliation and repentance go hand in hand. The pattern is the same: *In John's Gospel, wherever there is sin, Jesus addresses it.* (Remember what He said to the lame man He had healed? "See, you are well again. Stop sinning or something worse may happen to you" [John 5:14].) It's all part of the confrontational message.

Look at the Lord's words in John 8:

> ...if you do not believe that I am [He], you will indeed die in your sins. ... I tell you the truth, everyone who sins is a slave to sin. ... So if the Son sets you free, you will be free indeed. (John 8:24,34,36)

Those who do not believe will die in their sins; those who believe are set free. There are slaves of sin and there are servants of the Son. There are prisoners of darkness and there are people of light. For John (that is, for the Jesus whom John presents), *believing* means *turning* from darkness to light and from sin to the Savior.

This is the clear testimony of the entire New Testament. It is taught plainly in the epistles of Paul:

> For you were once darkness, but now you are light in the Lord. Live as children of light (for the fruit of the light consists in all goodness, righteousness and truth) and find out what pleases the Lord. Have nothing to do with the fruitless deeds of darkness, but rather expose them. (Eph. 5:8-11)

But it is taught even more plainly in the epistles of John. (That's right, in John!)

> If we claim to have fellowship with Him yet walk in the darkness, we lie and do not live by the truth. ... Whoever claims to live in Him must walk as Jesus did. ... Anyone who claims to be in the light but hates his brother is still in the darkness. ... Anyone who hates his brother is a murderer, and you know that no murderer has eternal life in him. (1 John 1:6; 2:6,9; 3:15)

So much for salvation without radical new life according to John!

Yet many people are confused when they hear that they must turn from their sins in order to be saved. "Doesn't that mean that salvation is by works instead of by grace through faith?" Not at all.

Repentance is part of the process of believing. It means a turning *toward* the light and *away from* the darkness; it means an about-face, a reversal. Instead of pursuing sin, you are now pursuing salvation. And when you turn away from your sin and turn to God, He pardons you freely. He takes away your sins! He pronounces you righteous through His Son. He washes you clean and gives you new birth. You are no longer a captive of the devil; you are a child of the King.

My friend, that's grace, not works! It is a gift, simple and free. You have not earned it at all. But this notion that someone can remain enslaved and imprisoned, blind and bound, unrepentant and unrenewed, *and yet be saved*, makes a mockery of the blood of Jesus. And it makes a mockery of the Gospel of John. Yet a New Testament Greek professor has taught this very thing in his popular book published by a leading Christian publisher. According to him, in John's Gospel there is:

> Not a word—not a syllable—about repentance... [Therefore] only a resolute blindness can resist this obvious conclusion: *John did not regard repentance as a condition for eternal life....* [God] does not *need* to...use repentance to draw men to saving faith in Christ.

Is it possible we are reading a different John? Maybe we have a different definition of repentance. According to this author:

> The call to repentance is *broader than* the call to eternal salvation. It is rather a call to *harmony* between the creature and his Creator, a call to *fellowship* between sinful men and women and a forgiving God.

> If we keep this fact firmly in mind, we will never make the mistake of thinking repentance is a condition for eternal salvation.

Now things are getting really bizarre. According to this definition of repentance, we can be saved without ever coming into harmony and fellowship with God. And what, pray tell, will we do in Heaven? Start a rebellion? Or maybe we repent on the way up!

How unbiblical to think that a man can live his whole life in darkness—before and *after* his "conversion"—yet, because he "believes" in Jesus, when he dies he enters into endless light. That is not what John's Gospel teaches us. According to John, those who believe are those who come into the light; those who remain in the darkness are still condemned. Repentance means coming into the light—in thought, word and deed. In the words of a young Chinese man who had embraced the gospel under the ministry of Jonathan Goforth: "The sins of my life have to go, since this Savior has come into it."

The act of faith may precede the conscious act of repentance, but where there is true faith, repentance is sure to follow. The *time* involved is not the key issue, nor is the *amount* of sin the question. But a good tree must bear good fruit, and true saving faith will *always* lead to a changed outer life. It cannot be divorced from repentance.

Some people have a problem with this truth. One mature Christian scholar—a greatly respected teacher who even has compiled his own study Bible—believes that he can prove it is unbiblical to expect people to completely repent of all their sins in order to be saved. (By the way, if someone *could* completely repent of their sins, then they wouldn't need Jesus! Still, let's listen to the argument anyway.) He gives this example from his own life. When some missionaries told him that sinners needed to fully accept the lordship of Jesus in order to be saved, he asked, "What about smoking cigarettes? Could someone be saved if they didn't stop smoking?" Reluctantly these missionaries replied that a person could *not* be saved if he didn't break his smoking habit.

Yet this argument cuts both ways. If we admit that every child of God struggles at times with total submission to the lordship of Jesus (who doesn't?) then where do we draw the line? If we can't expect people to abandon their lustful thoughts in order to be saved, maybe they can keep on reading pornography too. After all, nobody's perfect! So if they can be saved without giving up pornography, maybe they can continue to commit adultery with a different partner every week. Or maybe they don't have to turn from their homosexuality, or give up molesting children, or repent of being sadistic serial killers.... After all, nobody's perfect! *The very thought of such things is revolting.*

But it doesn't stop there. If it is impossible to draw the line of what exactly constitutes full surrender, maybe a person could believe in Jesus *and* in idols. Why is the sin of idolatry worse than any other sin? Why not believe in Jesus *and* Krishna? What about the sin of unbelief? Doesn't someone have to repent of *that* sin in order to be saved? Then if the sinner must repent of idolatry and unbelief, why doesn't he have to repent of his other known sins?

Of course, the message of repentance does not require sinful people to reach some level of spiritual perfection in order to be saved. Perish the thought! But, in the words of Dr. Edward N. Gross, although a person does not have to consciously accept Jesus as Lord in order to be born again:

> I, likewise, do not believe that a person can *CONSCIOUSLY OPPOSE* receiving Jesus as Lord and be a true Christian. Many have been truly converted without any knowledge of Jesus' Lordship. However, in my opinion, none have been converted who knowingly and deliberately resist the reign of Jesus in their souls.

Still, Gross continues:

> Having said this, however, I strongly believe that people ought to KNOW what they are doing when they come to Christ. The fact that people can be converted without the knowledge of Christ's Lordship should not determine our method of evangelism. The Holy Spirit does work mysteriously, sometimes, through very little knowledge of Scripture. But such are exceptional cases. And we should not allow exceptions to determine our policies.

If evangelists and soul winners would tell sinners the truth *up front*, then "follow up" ministry wouldn't be so frustrating, the process of discipleship wouldn't be so dreadful, and pastors wouldn't have to spend so much of their time later on catering to half-renewed rebels. (Or should we call them "semi-saved"?) How wonderful it would be if our contemporary campaigns actually yielded tangible evidence of a genuine work of the Spirit instead of multitudes of "decisions" any good salesman could produce. With the right music, lots of church co-ordination, careful advance planning, and a well-known, persuasive speaker, you can have yourself a bonafide, twentieth-century, made in the U.S.A., evangelistic rally. But with just one red-hot, eternity-minded, Spirit-anointed, no-compromise man or woman of God proclaiming the truth, you can have yourself a revival. Oh, that the Lord would raise up such vessels in our land in this hour!

*Anyone who truly turns to the Son will inevitably turn from sin.* It is biblical to preach this message at the very outset: "You can't have both the Savior and your sins! In fact, when you really met Jesus—in His beauty and majesty and grace—your appetite for sin will dissipate and disappear."

I can testify to this personally. In 1971, the battle for my soul began. On November 12 of that year, for the first time in my life, I *believed* that Jesus died for me. But I wasn't willing to surrender! For six weeks I struggled, attending church one night and shooting heroin the next. Then, on December 17, when the love of God penetrated my stubborn, proud heart, deep-seated strongholds of sin were almost instantly demolished. I was free to serve the Lord! Yes, the Light overcame the darkness, but it was a case of "either/or." Light and darkness can never mix.

That is certainly the message of John. Jesus said:

I am the light of the world. Whoever follows Me will never walk in darkness, but will have the light of life. (John 8:12)

He also taught:

Everyone who does evil hates the light, and will not come into the light for fear that his deeds will be exposed. But whoever lives by the truth comes into the light, so that it may be seen plainly that what he has done has been done through God. (John 3:20-21)

Let *each of us* come boldly into the light that our deeds may be exposed and made known. After all, we have nothing to hide. Do we?

*When I really enjoy God I feel my desires of Him the more insatiable and my thirstings after holiness the more unquenchable. O' this pleasing pain. It makes my soul press after God.*

David Brainerd

*I do not know when I am more pefectly happy than when I am weeping for sin at the foot of the cross.*

Charles H. Spurgeon

*If the cause be removed, the effects will cease. If the spring be purified, the waters will be healed, and the barren ground become productive.*

Andrew Fuller

*Never object to the intense sensitiveness of the Holy Spirit in you when He is educating you down to the scruple; and never discard a conviction. If it is important enough for the Holy Spirit to have brought it your mind, that is the thing He is detecting.*

Oswald Chambers

*For the word of God is living and active. Sharper than any double-edged sword, it penetrates even to dividing soul and spirit, joints and marrow; it judges the thoughts and attitudes of the heart. Nothing in all creation is hidden from God's sight. Everything is uncovered and laid bare before the eyes of Him to whom we must give account.*

Heb. 4:12-13

*"Is not My word like fire," declares the Lord, "and like a hammer that breaks a rock in pieces?"*

Jer. 23:29

# Chapter Seven

# When the
# Holy Spirit Comes

In 1907 there was a mighty outpouring of the Spirit in Korea. It came after months of prayer in 1906, and the breakthrough was dramatic. The churches had come to the end of the one united week of prayer in January 1907. Fifteen hundred expectant believers were now gathered together in the Central Presbyterian Church on a Sunday night, but...

The heavens over them seemed as brass. Was it possible that God was going to deny them the prayed-for outpouring? Then all were startled as Elder Keel, the leading man in the church, stood up and said, "I am Achan. God can't bless because of me. About a year ago a friend of mine, when dying, called me to his home and said, 'Elder, I am about to pass away; I want you to manage my affairs, my wife is unable.' I said, 'Rest your heart; I will do it.' I did manage that widow's estate, but I managed to put one hundred dollars of her money into my own pocket. I have hindered God, I am going to give that one hundred dollars back to that widow tomorrow morning."

Instantly it was realized that the barriers had fallen, and that God, the Holy One, had come. Conviction of sin swept the audience. The service commenced at seven o'clock Sunday evening, and did not end until two o'clock Monday morning, yet during all that time dozens were standing weeping, awaiting their turn to confess. Day after day the people assembled now, and always it was manifest that the Refiner was in His temple (Jonathan Goforth).

The results of that initial breakthrough were also dramatic. The Holy Spirit fell in power, and demonic resistance fell in pieces. Hard hearts were shattered, strongholds of sin were demolished, and the name of Jesus—not of any man, ministry or denomination—was exalted. How different all this is from so many of our "Holy Spirit meetings" today!

In the past, Holy Spirit meetings were often awesome; today they are largely orchestrated. In the past, there was conviction in the air; today there's a carnival atmosphere. There used to be lasting results; today there are lingering disappointments. Dare we say it is the same Spirit doing the same work?

In the past, when the Holy Spirit came, people would fall on their faces and then rise to their feet changed. Today they regularly fall on their backs and are helped to their feet *unchanged.* (The way someone falls is not the issue. It's what happens to their lives that counts.) What we think is supernatural is largely superficial; outwardly things may look exciting, but inwardly they are empty. Is this the Spirit, or is it a show?

Remember, the Holy Spirit hasn't changed. He is still holy. He still convicts of sin. He still comes to glorify Jesus. His presence still evokes holy fear. But today, when we are supposedly experiencing a mighty deluge of the Spirit here in America, when we are told that Joel's prophecy of a last days outpouring is reaching its final fulfillment, when preachers inform us that they are absolutely dripping with the anointing, there is hardly any holy fear. How can it be that God is so near and yet *conviction* is so distant? How can we claim such familiarity with the Holy One and yet be such strangers to holiness? Something just doesn't line up!

When the Holy Spirit comes there is conviction, contrition and confession. He sifts and searches, examines and exhumes. (That's right, He exhumes! He unearths unconfessed sins that we have conveniently buried out of sight.) He probes and pries, delves and digs. Nothing is left untouched. No one is left unchanged—for better or for worse.

When Peter—filled with the Spirit and separated to God—preached his message of repentance and judgment, the people cried out, "Brothers, what shall we do?" (Acts 2:37; A.T. Robertson explains that the rare Greek verb used in Acts 2:37 for "cut to the heart" means "to pierce, to sting sharply, to stun, to smite," just as a horse would dent and scrape the ground with its hooves. "The sermon went home. They felt the sting of Peter's words: compunction.") *If we—filled with the same Spirit and separated to the same God—preached the same message of repentance, warning and promise, we would get the same results.*

What torture cannot elicit, the presence of God can. Dr. Walter Phillips describes a scene that became common in revivals spearheaded by Jonathan Goforth in China:

> The very air seemed electric—I speak in all seriousness— and strange thrills coursed up and down one's body. Then above the sobbing, in strained, choking tones, a man began to make public confession. Words of mine will fail to describe the awe and terror and pity of these confessions. It was not so much the enormity of the sins disclosed, or the depths of iniquity sounded, that shocked one.... It was the agony of the penitent, his groans and cries, and voice shaken with sobs; it was the sight of men forced to their feet, and, in spite of their struggles, impelled, as it seemed, to lay bare their hearts that moved one and brought the smarting tears to one's eyes. Never have I experienced anything more heart-breaking, more nerve racking than the spectacle of those souls stripped naked before their fellows.

Here is a typical testimony from the 1907 Korean revival:

> Mr. Mackenzie, the war correspondent, had a boy who cheated him out of less than four dollars. That boy, when convicted, walked eighty miles and had a missionary send that money to Mr. Mackenzie (Goforth).

That is the convicting power of the Spirit! That is what happens when *God* touches someone's life. He touches them through the anointed Word!

From the soul-saving ministry of William Booth comes this eyewitness account of a truly evangelistic service:

> Penitent sinners have come up the aisle so overcome as to be hardly able to reach the rail. Fathers and sons, mothers and daughters have knelt side by side weeping. [Remember,

these were *lost sinners* coming forward to be saved.] ... The preacher was again earnest, *terrible*, melting, full of pathos. The Word was with power.

William Booth's wife Catherine describes another evening outreach:

> The communion rail was filled in a few minutes with great strong men who cried aloud for mercy, many as though the pains of hell had actually got hold of them. The cries and the shouts of the penitents almost overpowered the singing. At night there was a gale of saving grace.... The meeting did not finally close until 3 a.m. and the chapel was open the next day.

Or consider the great outpouring that occurred July 23, 1839, at Kilsyth, Scotland, during the preaching of William C. Burns. Under an overwhelming unction from on high, he pleaded with the unconverted to receive God's mercy *at that very moment* and, he says:

> I continued to do so until the power of the Lord's Spirit became so mighty upon their soul as to carry all before it, like the "rushing mighty wind" of Pentecost.

> They broke forth simultaneously in weeping and wailing, tears and groans, intermingled with shouts of joy and praise from some of the people of God. The appearance of a great part of the people from the pulpit gave me an awfully vivid picture of the state of the ungodly in Christ's coming to judgment. Some were screaming out in agony; others—and among these, strong men—fell to the ground as if they had been dead. This was the morning service, which, however, went on until three in the afternoon, and was only dismissed on the announcement of a resumption at six o'clock; and such was the general commotion that, after repeating the most free and urgent invitation of the Lord to sinners (as Isa.

55:1 and Rev. 22:17) I was obliged to give out a **Psalm**, which was soon joined in by a considerable number, our voices mingled with *the mourning groans of many prisoners sighing for deliverance.*

What a picture of the ministry of the Holy Spirit: Careless sinners and deceived believers suddenly see the staggering weight of their sin. They become totally undone. Their self-righteous arrogance falls to the ground. Their empty excuses evaporate into thin air. They stand **guilty** before an all-holy Judge. The pressure becomes unbearable. "Have mercy on me!" they cry. Then grace floods their souls and they are *free*. Really free!

Radical change must come. It is inevitable.

A man who had a wife and one son in We Ju [Korea] left them and became rich in another city. There he married another woman, and by her had two daughters. When his soul was revived he arranged for the support of this woman and her daughters, and went back to We Ju and was reconciled to his lawful wife (Goforth).

What tangible results the Holy Spirit produces!

When Goforth shared this example in 1936 at a meeting in Ontario, Canada, he added a striking comment: "*If the Korean kind of revival ever reaches some Christian lands, where divorce prevails, there will be some startling social upheavals.*" The mind reels at the thought of the social upheavals that would be produced by a real "Holy Ghost revival" in today's divorce-ridden America! And with a sky-rocketing divorce rate *in the Church*, how can we lay claim to any kind of deep visitation of the Spirit in this hour?

When the Holy God comes in holy power into the midst of His people, He begins His work by making them holy. But our typical congregations—rich in the flesh and abounding in sin—give little evidence of the abiding presence of the Holy Spirit, in spite of all our boasts.

Today, during the course of a so-called super anointed meeting, the preacher performs and struts; he pleads for money in Jesus' name or else uses sophisticated spiritual manipulation to continue funding his "ministry"; testimonies are given for the glory of man; and most of the people attending, pepped up by the high flying "worship" team and pumped up by the message, *leave just as they came*. Only their souls have been inflated. The flesh still lusts to sin and the spirit still longs to be satisfied. Conviction, transformation, rededication and fresh resolution are rarely seen.

In the past, in times of revival, believers came to church early and were consumed. Today we generally come late and are careless. They danced for joy; we mainly dance to the beat. They saw much and said little; we see little and say much. They were Spirit-reliant; we are self-reliant. They were respected for their sainthood; we are ridiculed for our scandals. They made their society Christian; our society has made us carnal. They were evangelists; we are entrepreneurs. They told exciting stories of sacrifice; we attend expensive seminars on success. Are we really *filled* with the same Spirit they were?

Goforth relates how one church in the new mission center of Shan Chun, Korea, experienced rapid growth in

1907. Although it broke off into five *new* churches that
year, its own membership grew from 870 to 1,445.

> *And no street radiating from that church had a heathen
> family left; all had become Christian.* Since they say in our
> Christian lands, "the nearer the kirk [church], the farther
> from grace," how do you account for that Korean church
> having no unsaved families near it? I can only account for
> it by the fact that they honor God the Holy Spirit, and there-
> by live such a powerful type of Christianity that all around
> them get convicted of sin, righteousness and of judgment.

What type of commitment did this kind of Christianity
produce among the ministers?

> After evangelizing the outlying islands of Korea they looked
> to the lands beyond. At the Presbyterian Assembly held in
> Seoul some years ago it was decided to send missionaries to
> Shantung, China. And when the call came for volunteers *the
> whole assembly rose and volunteered,* and four were
> selected. All seemed to envy the ones chosen. It has never
> been seen on this wise in a homeland assembly…. The sad-
> dest of all sad things is this, that the Almighty Spirit is as
> willing to let Christ Jesus see of the travail of His soul in
> Canada and the United States as in Korea, but He does not
> get the yielded channels.

In light of what the Holy Spirit has done in the past—
and what He desires to do today—only one question remains: Can He find a yielded channel in you?

*He that is merciful to sin is cruel to his own soul.*

Ralph Venning

*Jesus Christ came to make the great laws of God incarnate in human life, that is the miracle of God's grace. We are to be written epistles, "known and read of all men." There is no allowance whatever in the New Testament for the man who says he is saved by grace but who does not produce the graceful goods. Jesus Christ by His Redemption can make our actual life in keeping with our religious profession.*

Oswald Chambers

*Cheap grace is grace without discipleship, grace without the cross, grace without Jesus Christ, living and incarnate. Costly grace is the treasure hidden in the field; for the sake of it a man will gladly go and sell all that he has. It is the pearl of great price to buy which the merchant will sell all his goods. It is the kingly rule of Christ, for whose sake a man will pluck out the eye which causes him to stumble, it is the call of Jesus Christ at which the disciple leaves his nets and follows him.*

Dietrich Bonhoeffer

*For they superficially treat the fracture of My people saying, "All is well! All is well!"—when nothing is well.*

Jer. 6:14 (my translation)

# Chapter Eight

# Counterfeit Grace

There is a message sweeping through the Body today. Famous pastors are teaching it; best-selling authors are espousing it; leading theologians are defending it; *and the apostle Paul warned us against it*—three separate times.

To the Corinthians he wrote: "Do not be deceived" (1 Cor. 6:9). To the Galatians he wrote: "I warn you, as I did before..." (Gal. 5:21b). To the Ephesians he wrote, "Let no one deceive you with empty words, for because of such things God's wrath comes on those who are disobedient" (Eph. 5:6).

What was this great deception? What erroneous doctrine was Paul fighting against in such strong language and with such urgent appeals? It was the teaching that says, "Since you didn't do anything to earn your salvation, you can't do anything to lose it. No matter how you live, no matter what you do or don't do, no matter how far you walk away from God, if you're saved, you're saved. Otherwise grace would not be grace!"

But that is not grace according to the Scriptures. That is counterfeit grace, and it is producing what some have called counterfeit conversions. Jude also sounded the alarm, warning the saints in no uncertain terms:

> For certain men whose condemnation was written about long ago have secretly slipped in among you. They are godless men, *who change the grace of our God into a license for immorality* and deny Jesus Christ our only Sovereign and Lord. (Jude 4)

Of course, most of those today who teach the message of counterfeit grace are not "godless men" whose "condemnation was written about long ago," although, without a doubt, there *are* some charlatans and hustlers who have infiltrated our ranks and fleeced the flock of God. Woe to them on that Day! May they be exposed even now, while there is still time to repent and get right.

Such men—deceiving predators who parade around like devoted prophets—are the exception rather than the rule. Instead, good men and women, ministers dedicated in many ways to the things of God, Christian leaders who really do love the Lord, have bought into this doctrine, thinking somehow that it glorifies the Lord and liberates the saints. It does not! It stands in contradiction to the Scriptures and, in the name of grace, pollutes and sometimes even perverts the true meaning of the Word. Even though these ministers urge Christians to lead a holy life, (they do not openly condone sin!) their teaching opens wide the door to false assurance and loose living.

Look again at what the apostle Paul wrote:

> Do you not know that the wicked will not inherit the king-
> dom of God? *Do not be deceived* [That means the enemy
> will try to deceive us! But, as someone has said, being
> forewarned means being fore-equipped.]: Neither the
> sexually immoral nor idolaters nor adulterers nor male pros-
> titutes nor homosexual offenders nor thieves nor the greedy
> nor drunkards nor slanderers not swindlers will inherit the
> kingdom of God. (1 Cor. 6:9-10)

Could anything be more clear? Those who continue to
live wicked lives will not inherit the Kingdom of God. This
is not simply a matter of "going to Heaven but losing your
reward," as many have tried to teach. No! The *wicked* do
not go to *Heaven*. They have no reward to lose. So don't
be deceived! The professing believer who lives a wicked
life will not go to Heaven either. He will not inherit the
Kingdom of God.

Paul uses this very same language—"inheriting the
Kingdom of God"—to speak of the blessed event that
awaits the saints:

> I declare to you, brothers, that flesh and blood cannot inherit
> the kingdom of God, nor does the perishable inherit the im-
> perishable. Listen, I tell you a mystery: We will not all sleep,
> but we will all be changed. (1 Cor. 15:50-51)

That is what it means to inherit the Kingdom! It means
being changed. The perishable will put on the imperishable
and the mortal will put on the immortal. But the wicked
will not be changed. They will *not* inherit the Kingdom of
God. In other words, they will not be saved!

> He who overcomes will inherit all this [i.e., the new Jeru-
> salem filled with the presence of God and the spring of the
> water of life], and I will be his God and he will be My son.

> But the cowardly, the unbelieving, the vile, the murderers, the sexually immoral, those who practice magic arts, the idolaters and all liars—their place will be in the fiery lake of burning sulfur. This is the second death. (Rev. 21:7-8)

Amazingly enough, one of the most influential preachers in England, quoted earlier in this book, argues:

> The warnings of Paul relative to the kingdom of God do not remotely relate to being saved but to something else, namely, the *conscious presence of God*.... It is not salvation, then, but their inheritance in the kingdom of God that these Christians [whom Paul was warning] were in danger of forfeiting.

Yet it is folly to argue that the sin of a "Christian" idolater or adulterer will exclude him from the presence of God *here and now*, but will have no effect on his enjoying that same holy presence—in even more direct fashion!—forever. No. It is because the wicked are not at home in God's presence now that they will be barred from His Kingdom later. As Bishop J.C. Ryle explained:

> We must be saints before we die, if we are to be saints afterwards in glory.

"But," someone will ask, "who are we to judge what sins will keep someone out of the Kingdom of God? Who are we to judge who is wicked and who is not? We do not have the right to do such things." Of course we do! In fact, the Word does not only say that we have the right to judge, the Word also says we *must*. There is a world of difference between forming our own opinions about another believer (i.e., setting ourselves up as judges) and evaluating their lives by the Scriptures (i.e., judging them by the Word):

> But now I am writing you that you must not associate with anyone who calls himself a brother but is sexually immoral or greedy, an idolater or a slanderer, a drunkard or a swindler. With such a man do not even eat. (1 Cor. 5:11)

Such people will be excluded from the world to come, so we shouldn't make them feel at home in the local church. If they claim to be saved, but after having been confronted in a biblical manner (Gal. 6:1; Matt. 18) refuse to repent and live up to the most basic standards of godliness, then we are to *put them out of the Body.*

Listen again to Paul:

> What business is it of mine to judge those outside the church? Are you not to judge those inside? God will judge those outside. "Expel the wicked man from among you." (1 Cor. 5:12-13, quoting Deut. 17:7; 19:19; 21:21; 24:7).

> Nevertheless, God's solid foundation stands firm, sealed with this inscription: "The Lord knows those who are His," and, "Everyone who confesses the name of the Lord must turn away from wickedness." (2 Tim. 2:19)

The people of God are expected to live so differently from the people of the world that gross sinners will stand out clearly. (At least, that's what is supposed to happen! Today, instead of gross sinners standing out clearly, some of them stand behind pulpits boldly.) Our inheritance as saints is in "the kingdom of light" (Col. 1:12).

> ...For what do righteousness and wickedness have in common? Or what fellowship can light have with darkness? (2 Cor. 6:14)

We must "come out from [among] them and be separate" (2 Cor. 6:17). And if they are among us, calling themselves children of God while living hypocritical, unrepentant lives, we must put *them* out!

"But," someone will surely say, "what about grace?" Exactly! That is Paul's whole point. What about grace? Where is the evidence of grace? God's grace cannot possibly be at work in the heart of someone who ultimately refuses to turn back. Absolutely not. *God's grace does something.*

It is not just "unmerited favor," although anything we receive from God is through the merits of Jesus. "*G*od's *R*iches *A*t *C*hrist's *E*xpense" goes beyond forgiveness of sins. *God's grace means transforming power*. It means His holy influence on our hearts. It is an overriding work of the Spirit to make us like Jesus, converting criminals, sanctifying sinners, delivering drunkards, and renewing rebels. How wonderful is the grace of our God!

> For if, when we were God's enemies, we were reconciled to Him through the death of His Son, how much more, having been reconciled, shall we be saved through His life! (Rom. 5:10)

The grace that saved us from sin, cleansing us through the death of Jesus when we were not worthy, is the same grace that will keep us from sin, enabling us to live in victory through the life of Jesus, now that He has made us worthy. That is the power of grace. The pattern of our life is now victorious.

> For sin shall not be your master, because you are not under law, but under grace. (Rom. 6:14)

The law told you what to do and what not to do, without giving you the ability to obey. Grace changes your inner being so you supernaturally obey. The law is written on your heart. You delight to do His will. That is the grace of God!

This is how John Wesley explained the difference between his former "religious" state and his experience of the new birth:

> I was striving, yea, fighting with all my might under the law, as well as under grace. But then I was sometimes, if not often, conquered; now, I was always conqueror.

We are partakers of the Lord's victorious grace.

> For just as through the disobedience of the one man [Adam] the many were made sinners, so also through the obedience of the one man [Jesus!] the many will be made righteous. (Rom. 5:19)

Look carefully at this glorious verse: "The many" were not just called sinners; Adam's sin was not just imputed to them. Paul says they were *made sinners*. That is who they—and we—became: sinners! But, thank God for His incomparable grace, through the obedience of Jesus we have now been made righteous! Our very nature has been changed. We are not who we were, in deed and in truth. The grace of God has come, and it will "reign through righteousness to bring eternal life through Jesus Christ our Lord" (Rom. 5:21).

Yet some people still misunderstand Paul. They think he said, "Sin will no longer *condemn* you because you are not under the law but under grace." In other words, whatever

you do, there is no condemnation because you are under
the unmerited favor of God. That is not what he said, let
alone what he meant. No. He said, "For sin shall not be
*your master*, because you are not under law, but under
grace" (Rom. 6:14). The reason "there is now no condemnation for those who are in Christ Jesus" (Rom. 8:1) is
simply "because through Christ Jesus the law of the Spirit
of life set [us] free from the law of sin and death" (Rom.
8:2).

Jesus' death set us free! Gloriously free! Free from the
law of sin and death! Free to be a slave to righteousness!
Free to walk and live in the Spirit! Free to submit to God!
That is the message of grace.

Yet counterfeit grace is cheap grace, not because it *cost*
Jesus any less (in that sense there is no such thing as "cheap
grace"), but because it *does* less. It seals without sanctifying and redeems without regenerating, writing the sinner's
name in the Lamb's book of life while he continues to live
in death. (Remember, "The mind of sinful man is death..."
[Rom. 8:6].) That is not biblical grace!

Of course, many sincere teachers are afraid of falling
into legalism, which is the real danger of setting up an external standard of holiness and calling people to attain to it
in the power of the flesh. Yet consider this: It was to the
Galatians, Gentile believers who had actually become
caught in the trap of seeking to be justified by the works
of the law, that Paul wrote these words:

> The acts of the sinful nature are obvious: sexual immorality,
> impurity and debauchery; idolatry and witchcraft; hatred,

discord, jealousy, fits of rage, selfish ambition, dissensions, factions and envy; drunkenness, orgies, and the like. I warn you, as I did before, that those who live like this will not inherit the kingdom of God. (Gal. 5:19-21)

Calling believers to live a holy life, to conduct themselves in a godly manner, and to keep their hearts pure, is not legalism! That is what God's grace is for; that is how His grace will always instruct us to live.

For the grace of God that brings salvation has appeared to all men. It teaches us to say "No" to ungodliness and worldly passions, and to live self-controlled, upright and godly lives in this present age. (Titus 2:11-12)

So many leaders in the Body today claim that those who preach repentance and who emphasize biblical standards of holiness do not understand grace. (One prospering pastor even called repentance preachers "sick"!) These teachers assert that the true message of grace excludes any specific rebuking of sin. For them, the pardoned pervert—who never turns from his perversion—goes to Heaven, and the child killer who says the sinner's prayer is saved—even as he stalks his human prey. That is not mercy; it is a monstrosity.

Make no mistake. *Sin can keep you out of the Kingdom of God—in this world and in the world to come.* The Word is perfectly plain:

We know that we have passed from death to life, because we love our brothers. Anyone who does not love remains in death. Anyone who hates his brother is a murderer, *and you know that no murderer has eternal life in him.* (1 John 3:14-15)

> If your hand causes you to sin, cut it off. It is better for you
> *to enter life* maimed than with two hands *to go into hell,*
> where the fire never goes out. (Mark 9:43)

Willfully continuing in sin, in defiant disobedience to your
Maker, could cost you eternal life and secure you a place
in hell. The wages of sin is still death (Rom. 6:23)!

> I am quite sure that the root of nine-tenths of all the heresies
> that have ever afflicted the Christian Church, and are the
> cause of the weakness of so much popular Christianity, is
> none other than the failure adequately to recognize the
> universality, and the gravity of transgression. If a word
> comes to you, calls itself God's message, and does not start
> with man's sin, nor put in the forefront of its utterances the
> way by which the dominion of that sin can be broken in your
> own heart, and the penalties of that sin in your present and
> future life can be swept away, it is condemned—"ipso facto"
> (in the very fact itself)—as not a gospel from God, or fit for
> men (Alexander Maclaren).

Let me speak plainly to those of you who have swal-
lowed the lie of counterfeit grace, believing somehow that
"you are covered" no matter what you do. Hear me carefully. (Actually, hear what the *Word of God* says clearly.)
If you are walking in willful disobedience to God, if the
consistent and dominant pattern of your life (not the exception, but the rule; not a momentary lapse, but your actual
life style) can be described by any of the acts of the sinful
nature Paul listed in First Corinthians, Galatians or
Ephesians, then you must *question your salvation.*

Wake up! Get right with God! Turn back to Him now
while He is still calling you. Receive forgiveness and grace.
Be renewed in the spirit of your mind. Cast off the old man

and his ways. Walk in the Holy Spirit. He will give you the strength!

> Those who belong to Christ Jesus have crucified the sinful nature with its passions and desires. (Gal. 5:24)

I urge you in the name of the Lord: *Do not listen to those who lead you astray.* It is one thing to argue that if a person is truly saved, he will persevere in holiness until the end. In other words, if he falls, it will be only a temporary fall. He will prove his election by getting back up and going on with the Lord. (Whether or not that particular doctrine—called the perseverance of the saints—is taught in the Bible, at least it has this merit: It does not give out false assurance to the hardened backslider.) It is another matter entirely—in fact, it is absolutely criminal—to comfort the hell-bound with hollow promises of grace.

> But now He has reconciled you by Christ's physical body through death to present you holy in His sight, without blemish and free from accusation—*if you continue in your faith, established and firm, not moved from the hope held out in the gospel....* (Col. 1:22-23)

> We have come to share in Christ *if we hold firmly till the end the confidence we had at first.* (Heb. 3:14)

The apostle is sounding an alarm:

> For of this you can be sure: No immoral, impure or greedy person—such a man is an idolater—has any inheritance in the kingdom of Christ and of God. *Let no one deceive you with empty words....* (Eph. 5:5-6)

Empty words! Like these, from a concerned teacher:

[There is absolutely nothing] I can do about regeneration once I have experienced it. By that astonishing miracle I am constituted a child of God. Even if I were to decide I did not want to be His child, it would do me no good. My spiritual birth, like my physical one, is irreversible.... Of course, our faith in Christ *should* continue. But the claim that it absolutely must, or necessarily does, has no support at all in the Bible.

Or like these, from a concerned author:

It is possible, even probable, that when a believer out of fellowship falls for certain types of philosophy, if he is a logical thinker, he will become an "unbelieving believer." Yet believers who become agnostics are still saved; they are still born again. You can even become an atheist; but if you once accept Christ as saviour, you cannot lose your salvation, even though you deny God.

Or like these, from a concerned pastor and theologian:

I state categorically that the person who is saved—who confesses that Jesus is Lord and believes in his heart that God has raised him from the dead—will go to heaven when he dies, no matter what work (or lack of work) may accompany such faith. In other words, no matter what sin (or absence of Christian obedience) may accompany such faith.

No!

Let no one deceive you with empty words, for because of such things God's wrath comes on those who are disobedient. [This is not just a matter of "losing your reward." This is a matter of suffering the wrath of God that comes on the disobedient!] *Therefore do not be partners with them.* (Eph. 5:6-7)

Otherwise His wrath will come on you.

*Satan gives Adam an apple, and takes away Paradise. Therefore in all temptations let us consider not what he offers, but what we shall lose.*

Richard Sibbes

*What lust is so sweet or profitable that it is worth burning in hell for? Is any lust so precious in thy eye that thou canst not leave it behind thee, rather than fall into the hands of God's justice?*

William Gurnall

*The wages that sin **bargains** with the sinner are life, pleasure, and profit; but the wages it **pays** him are death, torment, and destruction.*

Robert South

*Sin, carried far enough, becomes its own punishment.*

Samuel Annesley

*The aged earth aghast*
*With terror of that blast*
*   Shall from the surface to the center shake,*
*When, at the world's last session,*
*   The dreadful Judge in middle air shall spread*
*His throne.*

John Milton

*You brood of vipers! Who warned you to flee from the coming wrath?*

John the Baptist, Matt. 3:7

# Chapter Nine

# The Wrath of God

The year was A.D. 79. Pompeii, one of Rome's most beautiful cities, sat at the foot of Mount Vesuvius. Children ran outdoors and played. Servants waited on their wealthy masters. Prostitutes plied their ever-thriving trade. Yes, all was normal in the prosperous city of Pompeii.

But under the earth, out of sight and out of mind, something was building. Countless tons of subterranean forces were about to collide. The pressure below mounted by the second....

And then, suddenly, it was too late! The ground shook, the mountain exploded, the sky lit up, and a river of fire gushed out. Blazing lava of two thousand degrees raced toward the sinful city, swallowing up everything in its path. It showed no mercy. It stopped for no one. It was a flood of liquid death.

Mt. Vesuvius roared and belched out smoke. A cloud of ash embalmed the newly dead. Seconds before they were the living! Everywhere there was panic; mothers screaming out, old men trying to run, toddlers crushed underfoot. But the screams were quickly silenced, since only those with breath can scream. The fire had burned up the air in their lungs!

Yet Vesuvius was a just a little volcano on a tiny planet called Earth. *One day the whole universe will erupt.* Consider the wrath of God.

> I watched as he opened the sixth seal. There was a great earthquake. The sun turned black like sackcloth made of goat hair, the whole moon turned blood red, and the stars in the sky fell to earth, as late figs drop from a fig tree when shaken by a strong wind. The sky receded like a scroll, rolling up, and every mountain and island was removed from its place. Then the kings of the earth, the princes, the generals, the rich, the mighty, and every slave and every free man hid in caves and among the rocks of the mountains. They called to the mountains and the rocks, "Fall on us and hide us from the face of Him who sits on the throne and from the wrath of the Lamb! For the great day of their wrath has come, and who can stand?" (Rev. 6:12-17)

But the judgment of God is not only a future event. His wrath is *already* being revealed. Look carefully at Romans 1:18-32.

There is a revelation of God in nature:

> For since the creation of the world God's invisible qualities—His eternal power and divine nature—have been clearly seen, being understood from what has been made, so that men are without excuse. (Rom. 1:20)

The autumn colors remind of us His creativity and love. The spring flowers tell us He is a God of vitality and joy.

The snow-covered mountains remind us that He reigns. But earthquakes tell us something too. So do hurricanes and tornados, tidal waves and volcanos, peals of thunder and flashes of lightning. They speak of the anger of the Lord.

> God is a righteous judge, *a God who expresses His wrath every day.* (Ps. 7:11)

When the land of Canaan became defiled because of sexual immorality and perversion, God "punished it for its sin, and the land *vomited out* its inhabitants" (Lev. 18:25). So to Israel the Lord said:

> And if you defile the land, it will *vomit you out* as it vomited out the nations that were before you. (Lev. 18:28)

Is it more than an ironic coincidence that the tragic and devastating mud slides in Rio de Janeiro in 1988 immediately followed the annual Carnival celebration, the world's largest homosexual orgy? Is there a reason there have been more major earthquakes in the past 50 years than in the past 2,000? Is the earth, defiled by centuries of abominable acts, *vomiting us out*? Is God speaking to us through nature?

Some will actually argue that "all storms and natural disasters are of the devil," pointing to the account in the Gospels where Jesus *rebuked* the wind and the waves. But that is a pitifully weak argument. What about the many times in the Old Testament where it was *the Lord* who, in judgment, sent hail and thundered earthquake or storm? What about Isaiah 29:6?

> The Lord Almighty will come with thunder and earthquake and great noise, with windstorm and tempest and flames of a devouring fire.

What about the New Testament description of God's throne in the Book of Revelation, surrounded by "lightning, rumblings and peals of thunder" (see Rev. 4:5; 8:5; 11:19)? What about Revelation 16:17-18?

> The seventh angel poured out his bowl into the air, and out of the temple came a loud voice from the throne, saying, "It is done!" Then there came flashes of lightning, rumblings, peals of thunder and a severe earthquake. No earthquake like it has ever occurred since man has been on earth, so tremendous was the quake.

Where did this angel come from?

> I saw *in heaven* another great and marvelous sign: seven angels with the seven last plagues—last, because with them *God's wrath* is completed. ... *Out of the temple* came the seven angels with the seven plagues.... And the temple was filled with smoke from the glory of God and from His power, and no one could enter the temple until the seven plagues of the seven angels were completed. (Rev. 15:1,6,8)

His wrath is actually glorious! Yet we have either ignored it, eliminated it, downplayed it or denied it.

Jesus spoke about judgment and hell *frequently*, and in terrifying terms. We speak of it *infrequently* (if at all) and then in watered down terms. Our loving and merciful Savior taught about Gehenna far more than He taught about Heaven, following the pattern of the whole Word of God. Yet the modern Church has not faithfully followed this Word. Are we smarter than the Lord? Are today's preachers more inspired than the authors of the Scriptures?

Here is a test for you. According to the Scriptures, fill in the blank: God says, "I will pour out My _____ ."

What is your answer? What was your first reaction? Did you say, "Spirit"? Then at least 75 percent of the time you were wrong! More than three out of every four times in the Bible, when the Lord says, "I will pour out My _____ ," He is speaking of His *wrath, anger* and *fury.* That is emphasized far more than the glorious outpouring of His Spirit, especially in passages dealing with the last days. The wrath of God is here, and the wrath of God is coming!

Why don't *we* emphasize these truths? Why don't *we* line up with the living Word? Are we more balanced than the Bible? Is it simply that we do not believe? Or maybe we're embarrassed, actually ashamed of the character of the Lord. We are in need of a spiritual overhaul!

How important is it for us to understand the wrath of God? Listen to Moses in the Psalms:

> Who knows the power of Your anger? For Your wrath is as great as the fear that is due You. (Ps. 90:11)

The reverent fear that is due Him is *great*!

Think back again to Revelation 6:12-17. Sinners would rather be crushed to death by rocks than even *see* the face of God. They would rather pray for an avalanche than have to deal with the Lamb in His wrath. And to the extent that His fire will consume the ungodly and His anger destroy the wicked—to that extent He is to be feared! Suffering the fury of the Lord is a fate far more terrible than the worst death (see Luke 17:2).

How staggering and overpowering is the thought of His holy wrath! (Ask the prophets: Jer. 4:19; 23:19; Is. 21:3-4;

22:4.) But we sleep on, or laugh on, or party on—unmoved and unshaken. May God give us eyes to see!

We have virtually eliminated the wrath of God from our theology and excluded it from our preaching, practically taking hell and judgment out of the gospel. We don't speak of it in church; after all, these people are already saved! Why teach them such "negative" truths? We don't speak of it in the world; after all, these poor, rejected, hurting people only need to hear about God's love!

Yet many of us are caught up in this present world. We put off judgment as an "eschatological event." We think of the lake of fire as if it were somewhere in Narnia. It seems too abstract, too distant, too farfetched. Then maybe this will wake us up: There is not only a revelation of God's wrath in nature, there is a revelation of His wrath *even now* in our society.

> The wrath of God is being revealed from heaven against all the godlessness and wickedness of men who suppress the truth by their wickedness. (Rom. 1:18)

It can be measured with precision. Exactly how much wrath has already been revealed against America?

The first step in every civilization that falls away from the Lord is this: Although we knew God as a nation, we "neither glorified Him as God nor gave thanks to Him, but [our] thinking became futile and [our] foolish hearts were darkened." We became fools in our supposed wisdom "and exchanged the glory of the immortal God for images made to look like mortal man [superstars! sex symbols! "idols!"] and birds and animals and reptiles" (Rom. 1:21-23).

As a result, and as the first definite revelation of His wrath:

> Therefore God gave [us] over in the sinful desires of [our] hearts to sexual impurity for the degrading of [our] bodies with one another. (Rom. 1:24)

That is the judgment of God! *The so-called sexual revolution is the result of God's wrath.* He gave us over to degrading lustful acts. Promiscuity, pornography and "free sex" are curses rather than blessings. They defile the human race. But it gets worse!

We "exchanged the truth of God for a lie, and worshiped and served created things rather than the Creator" (Rom. 1:25). What a description of modern, pleasure-crazed America! So, because of this, "God gave [us] over to shameful lusts" (Rom. 1:26a)—lesbianism and homosexuality! That is the next stage in the revelation of His wrath. That is the next indication that He has given our nation over to judgment.

> ...Even [our] women exchanged natural relations for unnatural ones. In the same way the men also abandoned natural relations with women and were inflamed with lust for one another. Men committed indecent acts with other men, and received in themselves *the due penalty* for their perversion. (Rom. 1:26-27)

Could this be applied to AIDS? But there is still more!

> Furthermore, since [we] did not think it worthwhile to retain the knowledge of God [what a description of secular humanism!], He gave [us] over to a depraved mind, to do what ought not to be done. [We] have become filled with every kind of wickedness, evil, greed and depravity. [We]

are full of envy, murder, strife, deceit and malice. [We] are gossips, slanderers, God-haters, insolent, arrogant and boastful; [we] invent ways of doing evil [how about computer-porn, dial-a-porn, and pay-per-view-porn?]; [we] disobey [our] parents; [we] are senseless, faithless, heartless [murdering the fruit of the womb], ruthless [there are hundreds of serial killers in our land]. (Rom. 1:28-31)

Yet even this is not the end. There is one final sign in the revelation of God's wrath in society. It is this:

Although [sinners] know God's righteous decree that those who do such things deserve death, they not only continue to do these very things but also approve of those who practice them. (Rom. 1:32)

Yes, America has hit bottom. Perverts are now privileged. Abortion activists are adored. AIDS-stricken homosexuals are heroes. *We venerate the degenerate.* People of God awake! The judgment is already here!

When a nation slaughters almost 30 million of its precious unborn, judgment is already here! When radical feminists are elected to public office, judgment is already here! When homosexuals march through our cities, accompanied by our mayors, proclaiming, "God is gay," and "We want your boys," judgment is already here! When 100,000 of our young people carry guns to school, judgment is already here! When we have become the world's greatest debtor nation, when new diseases outpace new cures, when homeless children roam the streets, judgment is already here! When there is one murder every half hour and one reported rape every hour, when the courts convict the innocent and acquit the guilty, judgment is already here! Then, as if all this were not already totally devastating, remember some of the significant events in 1992: the worst race riots of the century (Los Angeles), the most costly natural disaster in our history (Hurricane Andrew), and the election of America's first pro-abortion President since *Roe v. Wade.*

The anger of the Lord is already being revealed. He has given us over to our sin. He has abandoned much of our society to a depraved mind. But there is far more judgment to come!

Not only will the Lord abandon this perverse generation, not only will the wrath of God be visited on this sinful, rebellious planet through calamities, disasters, plagues and wars, but the return of the Lord will be a judgment event. God's wrath will be poured out on the entire earth when His Son comes again:

> ...the Lord Jesus is revealed from heaven in blazing fire with His powerful angels. He will punish those who do not know God and do not obey the gospel of our Lord Jesus. They will be punished with everlasting destruction and shut out from the presence of the Lord and from the majesty of His power on the day He comes to be glorified in His holy people and to be marveled at among all those who have believed.... (2 Thess. 1:7-10)

That is what we pray for when we say, "Lord, Your kingdom come." It will come with awesome wrath!

Yet there is one last display of the anger of our God. It is the final sentence on the damned, meted out at the great white throne, when both earth and sky will flee from His presence. Sinners will be cast into the fire of hell (Rev. 20:11-15)!

On that day there will be "weeping and gnashing of teeth" (Matt. 8:12; 13:42; 13:50; 22:13; 24:51; 25:30)—Jesus spoke of this often! The wicked "will go away to eternal punishment" (Matt. 25:46); they will awake to "shame and everlasting contempt" (Dan. 12:2). They will be cast "outside, into the darkness" (Matt. 8:12), where "their worm does not die, and the fire is not quenched" (Mark 9:48; Is. 66:24). The Lord will destroy their bodies and souls in hell (Matt. 10:28); they will perish (John 3:16) and be burned up with unquenchable fire (Matt. 3:12).

And the smoke of their torment rises for ever and ever. (Rev. 14:11a)

No wonder Jonathan Edwards could write:

The damned in hell would give the world to have the number of their sins one less.

That is the wrath of God.

*The greatness of a man's power is the measure of his surrender.*

William Booth

*I feel persuaded that if I could follow the Lord more fully myself, my ministry would be used to make a deeper impression than it has yet done.*

Robert Murray M'Cheyne

*He that loves a tree, hates the worm that consumes it; he that loves a garment, hates the moth that eats it; he that loveth life, abhorreth death; and he that loves the Lord hates everything that offends him.*

William Couper

*Nothing is more essential to an acceptable approach to God in the duties of His worship in general, and particularly in receiving the seals of His covenant, than a thorough and universal separation from all known sin.*

John Witherspoon

*I long for love without any coldness, light without any dimness, and purity without spot or wrinkle.*

M'Cheyne

*God alone sees the heart; the heart alone sees God.*

John Donne

# Chapter Ten

# The Power of a Pure Heart

It is one thing to avoid sin. It is another thing to hate it. It is one thing to fight, scratch and battle, only to barely *resist* temptation. It is another thing to utterly *reject* it. Are we engaged in a reluctant wrestling match with the world or are we repulsed by it?

Now is a good time for a spiritual checkup: Do we have the heart of the Lord, a heart that loves good and hates evil, or do we long to do what is wrong and hardly manage to do what is right? Could it be that something important is missing from our lives? Is there a deeper moral transformation possible for us as the people of God? Can the new birth *really* give us a new heart?

The answer is emphatically *yes*. To begin with, it is part of the fear of the Lord.

To fear the Lord is to hate evil. (Prov. 8:13a)

Do not be wise in your own eyes; fear the Lord and shun evil. (Prov. 3:7)

...The fear of the Lord—that is wisdom, and to shun evil is understanding. (Job 28:28)

> Come, my children, listen to me; I will teach you the fear of
> the Lord. Whoever of you loves life and desires to see many
> good days, keep your tongue from evil and your lips from
> speaking lies. Turn from evil and do good; seek peace and
> pursue it. (Ps. 34:11-14)

The fear of the Lord means a moral "about-face." It
produces radical righteousness!

A deep, reverential appreciation for who He is—an all-
holy, all-powerful, perfect judge—will lead to a renuncia-
tion of sin. "Do not be afraid," Moses said to the children
of Israel after they had been utterly devastated by the
awesome presence of God at Sinai, "God has come to test
you, so that the fear of God will be with you to keep you
from sinning" (Ex. 20:20).

That's why Abraham wasn't willing to trust the people
of Gerar. He said to himself, "There is surely no fear of
God in this place, and they will kill me because of my wife"
(Gen. 20:11).

There is no telling what people will do who do not fear
the Lord. Why shouldn't they sin without restraint? If there
is no ultimate Judge and judgment, why shouldn't they act
with total impudence? Why not eat, drink and party, if this
life is all there is?

The fear of the Lord corrects all that—in a hurry! But
that is only the first step. It goes deeper still. When we
recognize that we "call on a Father who judges each man's
work impartially" we will live our "lives as strangers here
in reverent fear" (1 Pet. 1:17). When we fully understand
that "nothing in all creation is hidden from God's sight

[and] everything is uncovered and laid bare before the eyes of Him to whom we must give account" (Heb. 4:13), then we will certainly watch our walk and guard our talk. Playing games will be out of the question!

But there is more to our walk with God than reverencing Him and avoiding sin because of who He is. There is something deeper. *We are called to become like Him.* We are predestined to be conformed to the image of His Son (Rom. 8:29). We are called to participate in His divine nature (2 Pet. 1:4)!

Yet here is an amazing thing: The believers who love to proclaim, "We are gods! We are partakers of His heavenly nature! Our spirits are recreated in His image!" are all too often the very ones whose lives are filled with worldliness, corruption, pride, covetousness, independence and arrogance. Their bold confessions have not saved many of them from all kinds of scandals and impurity.

No! Partaking in the nature of God means (to put first things first) escaping "the corruption in the world caused by evil desires" (2 Pet. 1:4). The "new self" we are called to put on is "created to be like God in true righteousness and holiness" (Eph. 4:24). Being "in Christ" really does mean "a new creation; the old has gone, the new has come!" (2 Cor. 5:17) Through the blood of the Lamb, we truly are "a chosen people, a royal priesthood, a holy nation, a people belonging to God, that [we] may declare the praises of Him who called [us] out of darkness into His wonderful light" (1 Pet. 2:9).

Glory and honor to the Lord! These are not just abstract theological maxims. *This is divine truth.* God calls us to have His heart. He calls us to share in His holiness. He calls us to shine His light. He calls us to wage war on sin.

Yet how can we confront that which we are at home with, that which we are fond of, that which we are attracted to, that which we inwardly desire? How can we rebuke those who publicly do the very things we have not privately renounced? Can we really bring conviction to those whose greatest sin is *doing* what we *dream* of doing? Certainly Jesus didn't live like that!

> You have loved righteousness and hated wickedness; therefore [don't ignore that word; the Scripture says "*therefore*"] God, Your God, has set You above Your companions by anointing You with the oil of joy. (Heb. 1:9, quoting Ps. 45:7)

This is what will set *us* above our companions: If we, *like Jesus*, love righteousness and hate wickedness, then our Father will honor us with a special anointing of joy. That is the anointing we so desperately need: an anointing of the presence of God, an anointing of the person of God, the holy oil of salvation *joy*.

Purity and joy go hand in hand. It is the *righteous* who rejoice and are glad (see Ps. 32:11; 33:1).

This is a key to spiritual power: We will have God's authority to the extent that we hate what He hates and love what He loves, when we no longer resist temptation only because of its consequences, but also because of its content. That is a mark of a truly Spirit-filled, Spirit-dominated life. We *delight* in doing the will of the Father without feeling deprived or dejected. The love of the world is no longer in us (1 John 2:15-17)!

Of course, we are not called to abandon the world and its needs, and many fine leaders today emphasize what is called "friendship evangelism": Love the sinner. Establish a relationship with your lost neighbors and associates. Do not look at them merely as statistics. Don't try to stuff the gospel down their throats with some high-powered sales techniques either. Instead, become their friends.

Amen—as far as it goes. But there's still one problem. The Word declares that friendship with the world is hatred toward God!

> Anyone who chooses to be a friend of the world becomes an enemy of God. (James 4:4b)

For many, "friendship evangelism" can be a trap of the devil. Instead of becoming a friend to worldly people, we become friendly with the world. Instead of living transformed lives that confront the world in its sin, we slip into compromised lives that conform to the sin in the world. We become accustomed to wrong, acclimated to evil, tolerant of impurity, indulgent toward immorality—whereas we should be glowing brighter and brighter, shining forth like the Son of God, becoming ablaze with *His* glory.

How we need God's light to burst forth! How we need a fresh immersion of divine grace! How we need to bear the image of the heavenly!

> The mark of a life governed by the Holy Spirit is that such a life is continually and ever more and more occupied with

> Christ, that Christ is becoming greater and greater as time
> goes on (T. Austin Sparks).

It is God's purpose that Jesus have the supremacy (Col. 1:18). He must reign supreme in our hearts!

This is one of the reasons our witness is often so ineffective: Our hearts are divided, our affections are split, our loyalties are torn.

> ...Every kingdom divided against itself will be ruined, and
> every city or household divided against itself will not stand.
> If Satan drives out Satan, he is divided against himself. How
> then can his kingdom stand? (Matt. 12:25-26)

How then can our "kingdom" stand, if our hearts are hot one day and cold the next, rejecting sin one hour and reveling in it the next, warring with the devil one minute and welcoming him the next? No wonder we can't drive him out! *Those who mingle and mix with Satan will never gain the mastery over him.*

But—how painful yet how true!—we really are in a struggle. No one said it would be easy! Peter spoke of "sinful desires, which war against your soul" (1 Pet. 2:11); James spoke of the "desires that battle within you" (James 4:1); and Paul counseled Timothy to "flee the evil desires of youth" (2 Tim. 2:22). It is only when we have "done everything" that we can stand (Eph. 6:13). But—how powerful and how gloriously true!—*we can stand.*

There is a place of victory for the children of God! There is a place of purity! God's grace is totally sufficient. He can enable us, each and every one of us, to do His bidding with passion, to pursue His will with joy, to follow

Him *wholeheartedly*. Jesus has risen from the dead! *In Him* we are raised too! His life has now become ours. It is "Christ in you" which is the hope of glory (Col. 1:27). Let's allow Him to live through us!

In the Old Testament, people were *clothed* with the Spirit and *gripped* by the Spirit (Judges 6:34 and 14:6 in the Hebrew). But we have also been *immersed* in the Spirit and *filled* with the Spirit. He now *inhabits* us! Clothed, gripped, immersed, filled—that is the equipping of the Lord.

In the Old Testament, people like Job "feared God and shunned evil" (Job 1:1). They were called to "love the Lord [and] hate evil" (Ps. 97:10), to "hate evil [and] love good" (Amos 5:15), and "to act justly and to love mercy" (Mic. 6:8). We are certainly not called to anything less. We have been given the very armor of God! He has clothed us with *His* righteousness.

Study the Word carefully; the armor we are called to put on is the armor God Himself "wears." We put on the helmet of salvation (Eph. 6:17), and so does He (Is. 59:17)! We wear the breastplate of righteousness (Eph. 6:14), and so does the Lord (Is. 59:17). He is the Man of war (Ex. 15:3). We are called to "be strong *in the Lord* and *in His* mighty power" (Eph. 6:10). We fight His battles in *His* strength. We go to war with *His* arsenal. Yes, the weapons we fight with "have divine power to demolish strongholds" (2 Cor. 10:4).

> For everyone born of God overcomes the world. This is the victory that has overcome the world, even our faith. Who is

it that overcomes the world? Only he who believes that
Jesus is the Son of God. (1 John 5:4-5)

Listen to the Spirit of the Lord!

There is a place He is calling us to, a place of refuge
and life. We have a divine invitation. He is saying, "Come
away from your effort. Come away from your striving.
Come away from the filth and the stench. Enter the hiding
place. Enter the strong tower. Enter the fortress divine.
Seek the face of God!

"Then *emerge* clothed with fire, clothed with power,
clothed with authority, clothed with the very nature of God.
Arise and scatter the enemy! Give chase to the devil and
his hosts! Confront the world and its sin. Speak up to
hypocrisy and pride. Renounce ungodliness and greed.
Rebuke immorality and murder. Reject the lust and the lies,
'and pursue righteousness, faith, love and peace, along
with those who call on the Lord out of a pure heart' (2 Tim.
2:22), through His grace that makes you stand!"

\*    \*    \*    \*

The Scriptures teach that "there are six things the Lord
hates, seven that are detestable to Him" (Prov. 6:16), but
"the Lord loves righteousness and justice" (Ps. 33:5a). Can
you say, "Amen, Lord! Yes! Me too! I have an undivided
heart"?

*A man who wants to work for God can find work, and nobody can stop him.*

D. L. Moody

*Lose not your confidence of making progress toward the things of the Spirit; you still have time, the hour is not yet past.*

Thomas à Kempis

*Remember that "difficulty" is a word which has not meaning when applied to Him: it is not in Heaven's vocabulary; power belongs to God. Look out of yourself and altogether upon Him.*

John Summerfield

*God delights to be fully counted upon and largely used. The deeper the need, and the darker the surrounding gloom, the more He is glorified by the faith that draws upon Him.*

C. H. Mackintosh

*The great thing is to be growing up unto Christ. The young Christian who is growing is more interesting and more helpful to others than the most advanced one who is stationary.*

J. B. Stoney

*I believe that for one man killed by overwork in the cause of Christ ten thousand die from laziness.*

Moody

# Chapter Eleven

# No More Excuses!

The confrontational gospel message begins at home. We must confront *ourselves* with uncompromising truth. Are we really producing lasting fruit for the Kingdom or are we just making a lot of noise?

Oh, yes, it's easy to be "busy" for the Lord, running here and there, going to meetings and special events, counseling, preaching, teaching, raising funds, doing good works, "ministering" with all of our might for Jesus. But (let the whole truth be told!) much of our ministry today is a concerted, sometimes frantic attempt to make up for the absence of the Spirit. We are trying instead of tarrying, working instead of waiting, doing instead of dying, sweating instead of seeking. Our "spiritual" ministry reeks of the flesh. *What the Lord does is holy, holy, holy; what we do is hollow, hollow, hollow.*

We produce much, but so little bears the mark of Jesus. We boast of great numbers, but so few have been born from above. We are filled with activity and hype, but where is the glory of the Lord? Where is the touch of Heaven? Oswald Chambers exclaimed:

> How much Christian work there is to-day which has never been disciplined, but has simply sprung into being by impulse! ... It is inconceivable, but true nevertheless, that saints are not bringing every project into captivity, but are doing work for God at the instigation of their own human nature which has not been spiritually determined by discipline.

According to Chambers, "we mistake panic for inspiration."

Yet flesh-instigated, flesh-empowered ministry is only half of the problem. There is another side to the story, a side of *in*activity and *in*action. It is what I call "prophetic elitism"—the danger of becoming so fed up with the contemporary gospel scene, so sickened by performing preachers and Hollywood holiness, so grieved by manipulating ministers who are greedy instead of godly, so hurt by scandals and shallowness in the Body, that we completely withdraw from church life while we wait for a *genuine* move of God. Many of us have become useless in the process! We have atrophied rather than advanced.

Oh yes, we are seeking the "deeper" things of God, the "meat" of the Word, the more "sublime" experiences of the Spirit. We've had it with the crass and the crude, with the immature emphasis (so we think) on outward things like signs and wonders. We've moved beyond all that! *Now we're sophisticated.*

Unfortunately, what we call "sublime" and "sophisticated" is often a subtle and unconscious rationalization for the absence of concrete, divine reality. We speak in great and lofty terms, but in the Spirit we carry a little stick. We judge our "hyperactive" brothers who are filled with their own works, but we are filled with our own words.

Where is the *manifestation* of God in our midst? Where is the *demonstrable* proof of our great maturity? How is our holy inactivity any better than the fleshly frenzy of others?

We must look into our hearts and evaluate our lives. Have we thrown out the baby (of the tangible power of God) with the bath water (of Charismatic craziness)? Are we making empty excuses for the lack of heavenly visitation? Or, even worse, are we deluding ourselves into thinking that we *are* enjoying a real moving of God, only this time it's intangible? The Lord forbid that we deceive ourselves any longer!

When Elijah stood on Mount Carmel and confronted the prophets of Baal, he knew his life was on the line (1 Kings 18:20-40). If God did not answer by fire, it was all over. There could be no tricks or sleight of hand. In fact, Elijah even made it *hard* on the Lord. He had water poured on his sacrifice—not once, not twice, but three times—in the midst of Israel's worst drought.

> The water ran down around the altar and even filled the trench. (1 Kin. 18:35)

Then Elijah offered a simple prayer.

> Then the fire of the Lord fell and burned up the sacrifice, the wood, the stones and the soil, and also licked up the water in the trench. (v. 38)

Yes! Yahweh answered by fire!

When all the people saw this, they fell prostrate and cried, "The Lord—He is God! The Lord—He is God!" (v. 39)

The people even helped Elijah slaughter the 450 false prophets. They were absolutely convinced!

There is something crucial to notice about this story. Elijah didn't say, "Did you see the fire? How many of you sensed that the Lord answered my prayer?" No! God answered *tangibly*. The fire really fell. It even burned up the water! There was nothing "sublime" about it. It was a demonstration of pure power. It was more than a flicker in the Spirit; it was an all-consuming flame!

Many of us don't like to emphasize God's power. We prefer the soft, quiet, gentle, inward workings of God. We are like the ultra-rich connoisseurs who go to posh parties and eat what are supposed to be delightful delicacies—but they are really paltry pickings. The gourmet cook serves up a pint-sized helping of some bland dish with a French-sounding name—and the cultured guests call it exquisite. As for me, I'd rather have a nice juicy steak. *Give me something with substance.*

Of course, there is a place for the soft, quiet, gentle, inward workings of God. (Just read First Kings 19:1-13.) In fact, the most important things that the Lord does in our private lives, and even in our public meetings, are often done in a soft, quiet, gentle and inward way. But eventually there must be evidence that God has acted; there must be a tangible change or a tangible answer. Otherwise we have deceived ourselves.

Enough with our spiritual rhetoric. Enough with our exalted talk. If Paul were here today, he would "find out not only how [we] are talking, but what power [we] have. *For the kingdom of God is not a matter of talk but of power"* (1 Cor. 4:19-20). What kind of power do *we* have?

When someone is sick, can we pray the prayer of faith with results? When the demonized are brought to us, does the enemy genuinely flee at our command? Is there concrete evidence that our spiritual warfare is working? When we cry out to God, does He ever answer by fire—*any* kind of fire? Does our preaching or witnessing bring deep conviction, *ever*? Where is our power in the Lord?

If the Lord is really at work in our *hearts*, where no human eye can see, can we point to the change in our *lives*, which every eye can see? Are we clearly becoming more like Jesus? Are we controlling our tempers, subduing fleshly lusts, and showing forth the joy and peace of the Lord? Are we walking in long-suffering and compassion, pouring our lives out for the lost? *Being conformed into the image of the Son of God is anything but abstract.* We will look as He looked—in terms of character—and do what He did:

> ...He went around doing good and healing all who were under the power of the devil, because God was with Him. (Acts 10:38)

Is God with us too?

Remember, God is the ultimate "doer of the Word."

> ...My Father is always at His work to this very day [Jesus said to His opponents], and I, too, am working. (John 5:17)

Could you even countenance the Lord being lazy? Yet we, *in His name*, are so often lax.

Of course, He is pleased that we have rejected the mass-produced, superficial substitutes for the gospel that dominate the American scene. He commends us for our sensitivity and honors us for our honesty. He is glad that we want to die to all ambition and be free from an external, goal-oriented life. But, in stark contrast to many flesh-powered ministers, some of us are so busy dying that we are no longer doing! We have gone from the carnal extreme of doing everything (without the unction of the Lord) to the pseudo-spiritual extreme of doing nothing—supposedly *because* of the unction of the Lord.

Brothers and sisters, this cannot be. A truly spiritual person will always be a doer of the Word in conduct and in character, in word and in witness, in miracles and in might. Jesus did only what He saw His Father doing (John 5:19), and what a life of doing He lived! It was no different with the apostles. As Smith Wigglesworth said, "The Acts of the Apostles was only written because they acted." God expects us to act too—with our eyes firmly fixed on Him, following only His orders and commands, equipped with His arsenal from on high.

Some will surely say, "I agree with everything you say. But what can we do now? We are *not yet* fully equipped, and if we pray for new souls and begin to invade our communities with the gospel, we'll do more harm than good. Our witness will be too flawed."

That too can be a great delusion. Our witness will never be perfect and we will never be perfectly equipped. In fact, most of us who are saved today are the fruit of some well-meaning, yet far from perfect Christian. What hinders us from bearing like precious fruit? Don't we have something wonderful, and crucial, to offer to every sinner today, in spite of the tragic condition of the American church?

What if the people who led you to the Lord chose to wait for greater Christlikeness instead of witnessing to you? What if they became so sophisticated, so sensitive, and so "tactful" (like many of us have become) that they never shared their faith with you? Where would you be today?

Oh yes, we want to do everything just right. We are so eager to be correct. But it's better to be alive than to be "correct." As Brother Andrew, "God's smuggler," once said:

> It's easier to cool down a fanatic than to warm up a corpse.

Better that God has to slow us down in our zeal than that He has to stir us from our lethargy!

It is true that some are held back by fear of deception. After all, many counterfeit miracles, lying signs and wonders, charalatans, impostors, and false teachers are both inside and outside the Body, right? "We need to be cautious," some would say. Besides, our heresy-hunting, spiritual watchdog brethren will always be there to warn of us impending error—if we deviate one iota from their self-proclaimed doctrinal norms, norms that would disqualify many of the great leaders in the history of the Church, as well as much of the earthly ministry of Jesus!

These well-meaning, but often overzealous guardians of the faith are swift to expose the flashy charismatic showmen who have the doctrinal stability of a skyscraper built on a foundation of jello. They are quick to quote the warning of Jesus in Matthew 7:22:

> Many will say to Me on that day, "Lord, Lord, did we not prophesy in Your name, and in Your name drive out demons and perform many miracles?" Then I will tell them plainly, "I never knew you. Away from Me, you evildoers!"

But they seem to have forgotten the words Jesus addressed to His disciples in Mark 9:38-40, when He rebuked them for trying to stop a man who was driving out demons in His name, but who was not "one of them."

> "Do not stop him," Jesus said. *"No one who does a miracle in My name can in the next moment say anything bad about Me,* for whoever is not against us is for us." (vv. 39-40)

He may not be "one of us"; he may not do things the way we're used to, or conform to our expectations, or follow our traditions, or belong to our denomination or group, or even hold to all of our sacrosanct doctrine, but if he's "not against us" then he's "for us"! (I know this may not sound precise enough for some, but I'm only repeating what the Master said.)

Yes, doctrine is important. Absolutely! It is utterly foundational. But who says every detail of what you or I believe is exactly right? Who says your congregation (or mine) has attained to perfect understanding? Only the arrogant or immature (or ignorant) will say, "All my doctrine—and only mine—is sound. You're right if you agree with me."

Still, some of us are so frightened of going against *"the norm"* (actually, it's the norm that is often wrong!) that we become spiritually stifled and stuck. That is not the Spirit of the Lord! *God does not put His children in strait jackets.* He abhors and despises dead orthodoxy.

Unfortunately, this "orthodoxy" is on the rise in our day. It is the traditionalist's response to "Spirit-frilled" foolishness. (That is on the rise too!) These careful critics, who are suffocatingly sound, justify their "ministries" in the name of "biblical accuracy" and "spiritual maturity." But so much of their criticism is actually over matters of style. Who says *their* style is right?

Michal didn't like David's style:

> As the ark of the Lord was entering the City of David, Michal daughter of Saul watched from a window. And when she saw King David leaping and dancing before the Lord, she despised him in her heart. ... And Michal daughter of Saul had no children to the day of her death. (2 Sam. 6:16,23)

There may have been a natural reason for Michal's barrenness; David probably didn't go near her the rest of her life! But there is a spiritual lesson here too: A critical, judgmental spirit will never bear fruit! It is cursed to remain in its own little world, putting down everyone else and failing to exalt the Lord.

> There are few sadder sights than that of an old man who has outlived his generation and his usefulness, but who, for some reason, still lingers on, staring with crusty disfavor at any servant of the Lord, however humble, who may be for

the moment in a place of prominence in the **Kingdom of God** (A.W. Tozer).

Some of us have grown old and crusty before our time. *Stagnating saints soon stink.*

The plain truth is we bring glory to the Father by *bearing much fruit*, thereby showing ourselves to be Jesus' disciples (John 15:8). What the Lord said to the apostles also applies to us:

> You did not choose Me, but I chose you and appointed you *to go and bear fruit* [this includes more than the fruit of the Spirit]—fruit that will last. Then the Father will give you whatever you ask in My name. (John 15:16)

Where is *our* lasting fruit? How have *we* shown ourselves to be the Lord's disciples? *The time for excuses is past.*

Yet for all who will be honest with themselves, for all who will arise from elitism and throw themselves into the fray, for all who will ceaselessly petition the God who still answers by fire—the time for holy action has just begun!

*According to the weight of the burden that grieves us is the cry to God that comes from us.*

Joseph Caryl

*Groanings which cannot be uttered are often prayers which cannot be refused.*

Charles H. Spurgeon

*It's not under the sharpest, but the longest trials that we are most in danger of fainting.*

Andrew Fuller

*God is not like men, who make large promises, but either through inability, or carelessness, or unfaithfulness, do not perform them; but will certainly be as good as His Word.*

Matthew Pool

*Man's extremity is God's opportunity. Jesus will come to deliver just when His needy ones shall sigh, as if all hope had gone forever.*

Spurgeon

*I never pray for more than half-an-hour.... [But] I never go longer than half-an-hour without praying.*

Smith Wigglesworth

*A long time out of Christ's glorious presence is two deaths and two hells for me. We must meet. I am not able to do without Him.*

Samuel Rutherford

*There is nothing that you can possibly need but you will find it in Him.*

Robert Murray M'Cheyne

*Jesus says: Console yourself, you would not seek me, if you had not found me.*

Blaise Pascal

# Chapter Twelve

# Seek Him Until...

Is your heart aching for more of God? Is there a deep longing within you that cannot be satisfied by a good meeting, an anointed message, or an exciting manifestation of a spiritual gift? Is the cry of your soul, "Lord, how long?" Have you reached the point, not once, but over and over again, of feeling that you can't live any longer without seeing the glory of God? Are you starving for more of Jesus?

The children of Israel became slaves in Egypt. Their lives were filled with hardship and were empty of hope.

> ...The Israelites groaned in their slavery and cried out, and their cry for help because of their slavery went up to God. God heard their groaning and He remembered His covenant with Abraham, with Isaac and with Jacob. So God looked on the Israelites and was concerned about them. (Ex. 2:23-25)

How much time went by? Ten years? Twenty years? Forty years? How many sighs ascended to Heaven? How many groans reached the heart of God? How many Israelite mothers cried themselves to sleep at night? How many children wondered, "Did our forefathers really know God?"

How many strong men prayed with tears—until the tears turned to bitterness and despair?

But all along the Lord took notice! All along He heard! Not a prayer was in vain. Not a sigh was uttered, not a tear was shed without our heavenly Father caring, without Him saying, "Soon." And when the answer finally came, the divine response to generations of desperation and suffering, it was overwhelmingly awesome in glorious display:

> Ask now about the former days, long before your time, from the day God created man on the earth; ask from one end of the heavens to the other. Has anything so great as this ever happened, or has anything like it ever been heard of? Has any other people heard the voice of God speaking out of fire, as you have, and lived? Has any god ever tried to take for himself one nation out of another nation, by testings, by miraculous signs and wonders, by war, by a mighty hand and an outstretched arm, or by great and awesme deeds, like all the things the Lord your God did for you in Egypt before your very eyes? (Deut. 4:32-34)

Nothing like the Exodus had ever taken place. Never before had the Lord so bared His holy arm. Never before was there such a manifestation of divine glory. But, according to the testimony of the Word of our God, and confirmed by the deep witness in the hearts of so many of His people, He will do something more in our day! We must seek Him until the answer comes, until revival explodes, until the visitation is here, until the work is done. We cannot quit before then.

> Ask the Lord for rain in the springtime; it is the Lord who makes the storm clouds. He gives showers of rain to men, and plants of the field to everyone. (Zech. 10:1)

Sow for yourselves righteousness, reap the fruit of unfailing love, and break up your unplowed ground; *for it is time to seek the Lord until He comes and showers righteousness on you.* (Hos. 10:12)

Bear up the hands that hang down, by faith and prayer; support the tottering knees. Have you any days of fasting and prayer? Storm the throne of grace and persevere therein, and mercy will come down (John Wesley).

That is the critical need for the hour. We must storm the throne of grace, approaching our Father with confidence, hanging on to His promises with tenacity, believing that what He said, He will do. "Lord, for an outpouring in our day!"

Then Jesus told His disciples a parable to show them that they should always pray and not give up. (Luke 18:1)

You need to persevere so that when you have done the will of God, you will receive what He has promised. (Heb. 10:36)

Let us not become weary in doing good [is there anything we can do that is better than prayer?], for at the proper time we will reap a harvest if we do not give up. (Gal. 6:9)

But sometimes it gets so discouraging! A couple of years ago, I was doing a live telephone interview on a Christian radio show in Los Angeles, talking with the host about the bankrupt state of the American church and our desperate need for revival. When the phone lines were opened up for calls from the listeners, a theme from the callers began to repeat itself: "I thought I was the only one who felt like this. I thought I was crazy. Why is it that we never see any of the famous TV pastors confessing their emptiness? Why don't our leaders seem to be broken?"

Then one woman called in. She said that *for 15 years* she had been crying out to God for more of His presence. She would go home from church deeply frustrated, and travail and groan in prayer. She knew that what she was feeling was right, but like so many others, she questioned herself. Finally, she and her husband went to the pastor. "We want more of God," they said. "We have a program," the pastor replied. "Go somewhere else." That was supposedly a "Spirit-filled" church!

But for this woman and her husband, and for many of you who *long* for the glory of God, I want to encourage you. The Lord has heard your prayers! The Lord has seen your tears! The Lord is about to move! In fact, a stirring is already here. Spiritual hunger is on the increase. Corporate prayer for revival is spreading across America. The people of God have said, "Enough is enough." And, thank the Lord, it is getting clearer. A great shaking is in our land!

Pastors who went through the motions for years, without ever asking a question—fulfilling their responsibilities, implementing new plans, watching their congregations grow, sharpening their ministry skills—have now reached a point of holy dissatisfaction. As with Oswald Chambers during his time of great searching, they too are crying out: "If what I have is all the Christianity there is, then the thing is a fraud!"

Believers who have been zealous for all kinds of good works for years, hardly ever raising a complaint—never missing Sunday school, faithful in daily devotions, witnessing on their jobs, reading the Word as a family—are now wondering about their very experience in the Lord. "There must be something more," they say. I believe that is what you are saying too! It is the work of the Spirit. *Now is the time to press in.*

Are you asking yourself the very same questions that K.P. Yohannan, president of Gospel for Asia, and a man who lives for missions, has asked?

> ...What about the vast network of Christian activities that so often preoccupy our hearts, hands and minds in the West? Don't our frenzied lives prove our piety? I cannot look at them without asking the critical question, from where does this current wave of activism spring?

> Will it pass through the fires of judgment? Is it the work of our hands and egos, or does it spring from the heart of Jesus? If your Christian service were to end today, would it make any difference in eternity?

The Lord wants your life to count. What is the *maximum* He could do through you?

Years ago, James Gilmour, missionary to Mongolia, penned these searching words:

> Do not we rest in our day too much on the arm of flesh? Cannot the same wonders be done now as of old? Do not the eyes of the Lord still run to and fro throughout the whole earth to show Himself strong on behalf of those who put their trust in Him? Oh, that God would give me more practical faith in Him! Where is now the Lord God of Elijah? He is waiting for Elijah to call on Him.

Dear believers, dear pastors and evangelists, dear fellow-laborers in the Lord: Don't devise a new plan! Don't work yourself into a fit! Don't react in the flesh! *No.* Seek the

Lord. Persevere in prayer. Stretch yourself out before the living God. He will make His marching orders plain!

How long should you seek Him? *Seek Him until*—until the deepest longing of your heart is satisfied, until He has visited your life with His presence and anointed you with His power, until you are a living witness to the glory of the Lord. *Seek Him until...*

For those of you who have had it with shady politicians and shallow preachers, *seek Him until*. If you have been wounded by anti-moral educators and stung by immoral evangelists, *seek Him until*. For those of you who can no longer endure the pain of seeing so many aborted babies and such a multitude of stillborn believers, *seek Him until*. If you have reached the end of your self and come to the limit of your own strength, *seek Him until*. Seek Him until He comes through! Seek Him until He comes!

> The lions may grow weak and hungry, but those who seek the Lord lack no good thing. (Ps. 34:10)

> Those who know Your name will trust in You, for You, Lord, have never forsaken those who seek You. (Ps. 9:10)

Your earnest prayers are making an impact!

The great upheaval we are witnessing today in the world and in the Church is largely due to the prayers of the saints. In the Book of Revelation we read:

> Another angel, who had a golden censer, came and stood at the altar. He was given much incense to offer, with the prayers of all the saints, on the golden altar before the throne. The smoke of the incense, together with the prayers of the saints, went up before God from the angel's hand.

Then the angel took the censer, filled it with fire from the altar, and hurled it on the earth; and there came peals of thunder, rumblings, flashes of lightning and an earthquake. (Rev. 8:3-5)

*Faithful prayer has a cumulative effect*. We don't understand all the reasons why that is so. We don't always need to know every detail of what is happening in the spiritual, unseen realm, or which spirits should be "bound" and which spirits "loosed." The key thing we must know is, there is a battle going on to keep us off our knees, and we are called to "fight the good fight of the faith" (1 Tim. 6:12). In other words, putting aside advanced techniques of spiritual warfare: Don't cave in! Don't stop believing! Don't stop praying in confident expectation! Something happens when you pray.

If, in the parable of Jesus, an unjust, irreligious judge finally granted the plea of a helpless but persistent widow, then, the Lord taught:

... will not God bring about justice for His chosen ones, *who cry out to Him day and night*? Will He keep putting them off? I tell you, He will see that they get justice, and quickly. However, when the Son of Man comes, will He find faith on the earth? (Luke 18:7-8)

The struggle is for your faith. *Persistent prayer is the ultimate combat zone*.

The Puritans understood the concept of the cumulative effect of prayer. They realized that the big things, the grand purposes of God, would not come to pass without long-term and dedicated corporate and private prayer. Israel would never be saved without it. The world would not be evangelized without it. The Church would not become spotless without it. A passing petition or a fleeting flight of intercession would not bring these things about. But no prayer of faith is ever prayed in vain.

Listen to Puritan author Thomas Goodwin:

> There is a common treasure of the church, not of their merits, but of their prayers. There are bottles of tears a-filling, vials a-filling to be poured out for the destruction of God's enemies. What a collection of prayers hath there been these many ages towards it! And that may be one reason why God will do such great things towards the end of the world, even because there hath been so great a stock of prayers going for so many ages, which is now to be returned.

What an antidote to discouragement! We are building on *whole generations* of prayer for national and international revival. These prayers have already ascended to the throne of God and been mingled with the fires of the heavenly altar. The vials of stored-up tears are about to burst!

No people has ever been closer to the end than we. No generation of believers has ever had more prayers prayed and more intercession offered up, *before we ever opened our mouths or poured out our hearts to God*, than our generation. The "peals of thunder" and "rumblings" (remember Revelation 8) are already being heard. A great stirring has already begun. *Now*—not tomorrow, not when our children or grandchildren are grown, not when we're all dead and gone—but *now* is the time to press in. Unprecedented events are unfolding around us. How tragic if we dropped out now!

In the 1930's, God spoke to a Japanese missionary in Manchuria to return to his homeland and call the believers to pray for three things: (a) that the Jewish people would be regathered to their land as a nation; (b) that Jerusalem would return to Jewish hands; (c) that Jesus the Messiah would return. The first two have come to pass. The third will surely follow! *If ever there were a time to persevere, it is now.*

No doubt, our nation is in a wretched state. No doubt, the world as a whole is growing darker. No doubt, our race staggers from disaster to disaster. The needs have never been greater. But this is not the time for depression and hopeless despair. It is the time for the Church to finally be the Church: the living embodiment of the Son of God, "the fullness of Him who fills everything in every way" (Eph. 1:23). It is time for the Lord to get Himself glory! He will gain glory through each of us. As Catherine Booth said, "The waters are rising, but so am I! I am not going under, but over."

> Therefore, strengthen your feeble arms and *weak knees.* [Could this have a double meaning? Could it also be a call to more prayer?] "Make level paths for your feet," so that the lame may not be disabled, but rather healed. (Heb. 12:12-13)

The world, whether it knows it or not, is counting on you and me. There is no other source that offers true healing, outside of the people of God.

Of course, the task before us is impossible. And whether we are fighting against the spread of pornography or working to alleviate world hunger, whether our burden is foreign

missions or home evangelism, whether our ministry is healing the sick or setting free drug addicts, there is only one
place to go: To your knees, saints! On your faces, children
of God! To the place of prayer, holy intercessors! Seek Him
always (see Ps. 105:4). Seek Him with tears (see Heb. 5:7).
Seek Him earnestly:

> O God, You are my God, earnestly I seek You; my soul
> thirsts for You, my body longs for You, in a dry and weary
> land where there is no water. (Ps. 63:1)

Hunger and thirst for the Lord. Long for Him with a
lovesick heart. Let it be known by your prayer life that you
cannot and will not live without more—radically more—of
God.

How will He respond?

> For He satisfies the thirsty and fills the hungry with good
> things. (Ps. 107:9)

> The poor will eat and be satisfied; they who seek the Lord
> will praise Him.... (Ps. 22:26)

> My soul will be satisfied as with the richest of foods; with
> singing lips my mouth will praise You. (Ps. 63:5)

> Those who look to Him are radiant; their faces are never
> covered with shame. (Ps. 34:5)

> But may all who seek You rejoice and be glad in You; may
> those who love Your salvation always say, "The Lord be ex-
> alted!" (Ps. 40:16)

Our God will never fail!

Here, then, is our Father's promise, a personal invitation
straight from the throne:

You will seek Me and find Me when you seek Me with all your heart. (Jer. 29:13)

Does anything hold you back? Respond in faith with the psalmist:

My heart says of You, "Seek His face!" Your face, Lord, I will seek. (Ps. 27:8)

I will seek You until You come!

*Oh that the Lord would saturate us through and through with an undying zeal for the souls of men.*

Charles H. Spurgeon

*No Christian is in a right condition, if he is not seeking in some way to bring souls to Christ.*

C. H. Mackintosh

*I cared not where or how I lived, or what hardships I endured so that I could but gain souls for Christ. While I was asleep I dreamt of such things, and when I waked the first thing I thought of was winning souls to Christ.... All my desire is the conversion of sinners, and all my hope is in God.*

David Brainerd

*We do not have a book of the "Resolutions of the Apostles," but because of spiritual power and Gospel triumphs, we have the "Acts of the Apostles."*

The Marechale
(William Booth's eldest daughter)

*I am obligated both to Greeks and non-Greeks, both to the wise and the foolish. That is why I am so eager to preach the gospel also to you who are at Rome. ... Yet when I preach the gospel, I cannot boast, for I am compelled to preach. Woe to me if I do not preach the gospel!*

Paul, Rom. 1:14-15; 1 Cor. 9:16

# Chapter Thirteen

# Go for Souls!

The church of America must come to a difficult conclusion. We must face the hard cold facts. *It's too late for our nation!* It's too late for moral reform; too late for a social transformation; too late for a return to the "good old days"—unless masses of sinners get saved. Otherwise there is no hope.

For too long we have sought to make ungodly people godly, without converting them from sin. We have tried to make immoral people moral, through words, actions and votes. But it won't work! It can't work! Those who are accustomed to evil *cannot* do good, unless the Lord grants them a new heart. We must go after the souls of lost men and women. That is the call of the Church.

Then why speak up at all? Why protest in front of abortion clinics? Why take a stand for moral issues? Why confront secular school systems? It's all part of the gospel. It's part of our role of being the salt of the earth and the light of the world (Matt. 5:13-16); of being a voice of conscience to a depraved society (Phil. 2:14-16); of challenging the godless with the standards of God. Yet it is only *part* of the gospel. *We are called to be fishers of men* (Matt. 4:19; Luke 5:10). Now is the time to awake!

For years we put our trust in the government. We hoped that the President would hold the line, that the right appointees to the Supreme Court would help stem the flood of unrighteousness, that a politically active church would turn our nation back. But we have been misled! *We have put our confidence in the flesh.* In our fight for religious rights we have subtly confessed, "In man do we trust." But government cannot save! Only Jesus can save. And He must be our message.

Oh yes, we *should* exercise our rights and vote. We *should* meet with our children's educators and write to our elected officials. We *should* pray for mercy on our nation (although the best we can pray now is the prayer of Habakkuk 3:2: "In wrath remember mercy").

How can we *not* do these things? How can we *not* speak out against the aggressive homosexual agenda? How can we *not* vote for candidates who will fight for the truth? (If it's right to *pray* for the salvation of elected officials once they are in office [1 Tim. 2:1-4] why not *vote* for godly candidates to get into office?) We are not called to roll over and die. We must stand firm for what is right.

But here is where so many of us have missed it. We cannot expect radical feminists, militant pro-abortionists, hate-filled racists, committed secular humanists, or degraded sexual perverts to respond to our call for morality. That would be like Satan showing sympathy or a demon feeling sorry. It will never happen. Our only hope, and the only hope of our nation, is for these ungodly sinners to become born anew. They need a change of heart. Their minds are foregone and depraved.

Then why confront them at all? Again, the answer is simple. It's part of our witness. It's part of the message of Jesus: Expose the sinner's sin and then tell him that there's a remedy. Show him his guilt and point him to the only door of hope. Make him see that he is *lost*, and then tell him how he can be saved. But don't expect him to see the light or to accept the standards of God unless his soul is converted. *Conversion of the lost must be our goal.*

Oh yes, there are other reasons for speaking up for godliness and morality. First, if we don't, things will only get worse. There will be no moral force to restrain the wickedness, no voice of conscience to slow the increase of perversion, no upward trend to resist the slide down. Second, we can still save lives by our sacrificial actions on the behalf of those who cannot fight for themselves. Third, we are obligated to warn sinners of coming judgment. That way they will have no excuse. Fourth, if we do not exercise our God-given rights, then we will have no one to blame when those rights all disappear, when the government declares gospel preaching to be illegal and forbids the reading of Bibles in our homes. No, if we do not stand tall today, we will cower and cringe tomorrow.

But so many of us have gotten confused! Because we have put so much energy and effort into affecting the standards and laws of our nation, we have forgotten that without

Jesus, without the intervention of God, without a move of the Spirit, we only strive with the wind. "The flesh counts for nothing," Jesus taught (John 6:63; He was speaking of natural, human effort). It is "the Spirit [that] gives life."

Yet we have fought the battle in the flesh. We have somehow thought that human effort could accomplish God's will. Never! "Flesh gives birth to flesh, but the Spirit gives birth to Spirit" (John 3:6). Only the Spirit can do the work. Only the Spirit can everlastingly change lives. It is the ministry of the Holy Spirit that we need. It is Spirit-led, Spirit-anointed and Spirit-empowered praying, preaching, parenting, and witnessing that we must have today. That alone can shake our country.

Consider what we have done. When pro-abortion candidates were elected, we mourned (and rightly so). When the Supreme Court failed to overturn *Roe v. Wade* we were disappointed (and with good reason). When President Clinton signed radical pro-abortion legislation *his second day in office*, we grieved. (What true believer wouldn't?) But what else could we expect? Our preachers have not called our society to account, our pulpits have not sounded the alarm, our churches have hardly impacted their cities, and we have not individually "[lived] such good lives among the pagans that, though they accuse [us] of doing wrong, they may see [our] good deeds and glorify God on the day He visits us" (1 Pet. 2:12). And where the gospel has been declared, it has largely been rejected. Of course everything is crumbling around us! Our nation has abandoned God and He has abandoned us. There is only one possible course from here.

It's time for a change in strategy. It's time for a whole new outlook. Without retreating, without backing down, without giving up, without losing ground, we must come to a resolution: No more leaning on the help of man! No more trusting in the arm of flesh! No more claiming special rights because of our nation's blessed heritage! No more exalting our Constitution! It's time to exalt the Word. It's time to preach the gospel. It's time to go after the lost. It's time to reach out and be counted. Let us impact our nation through the cross! Our strength is not in who we know in the halls of Congress, it is in who we know in the courts of Heaven. It's the Savior, not the Senate, whom we trust! "Believe in God, not in government," is certainly an apt word for evangelicals in America.

Social action is necessary and good; but spiritual action is better. (It is not a matter of "either/or"; I am speaking of the issue of *priorities*.) Signing petitions has its place. (Remember the Preface to this book?) But street preaching can shake the place! Balloting is one thing; brokenness is another. The demands of organized protests reach the inner corridors of the White House. The voice of agonized prayer reaches the throne of God! Who is it we really want to influence? Whose favor do we covet the most?

The Lord is more interested in the Church than in Congress. True hunger for revival counts more with Him than the House of Representatives does. Christians carry more weight than Congressmen. But we must carry our weight where it counts!

Rather than trying to pressure the ungodly into morality, we should seek to pray them into ministry. Instead of making efforts to get blind sinners to see things our way, we should evangelize them until they see *the* Way. Intercession is better than intimidation. Fasting is more effective than fighting. Weeping does more than voting. Touching *God* is what really counts. Then we can touch the world, and touch the world we must!

> ...Go into all *the world*.... (Mark 16:15)

> For God so loved *the world*.... (John 3:16)

> He is the atoning sacrifice for our sins, and not only for ours but also for the sins of *the whole world*. (1 John 2:2)

> That God was reconciling *the world* to Himself...And He has committed to us the message of reconciliation. We are therefore Christ's ambassadors, as though God were making His appeal through us. We implore you on Christ's behalf: Be reconciled to God. (2 Cor. 5:19-20)

What an awesome calling! What a glorious privilege! We are the ambassadors of the Messiah and Lord! The living God makes His appeal *through us.*

Is that how we live? Is that what moves and motivates us? Is that what inspires our action and controls our conduct? Do we understand that we are Jesus' earthly representatives, His appointed agents, His designated envoys, His hand-picked emissaries? Are we dominated and driven by *His* mission?

The Savior of the world now lives His life through us. He expresses His heart for humanity through us. He who lived, bled, died, and rose for souls—for the lost, the ungodly, the sinful, the depraved—calls us to follow His example. "Be fishers of men!"

But, as far as spiritual activities are concerned, we are so internalized! So much of our spiritual energy is exerted on ourselves. Our church programs and ministries are oriented toward a "bless me, help me, counsel me, comfort me" mentality. We love the Christian talk shows that help us to *look in*. We thrive on the inner healing books that tell us to *look back*. But the Holy Spirit is urging us to *look out*.

> I tell you, open your eyes and look at the fields! They are ripe for harvest. (John 4:35b)

Yet, like migratory herds searching for greener pastures, we graze from church to church and ministry to ministry, upset with the praise and worship here, frustrated with the youth minister there, annoyed by the lack of love almost everywhere, and always offended by any message that would dare insinuate that something might be wrong with us. All the while precious souls perish by the minute! How the heart of the Savior must grieve.

At the end of the last century, William Booth preached a series of three great meetings at the Town Hall in Sydney, Australia.

> At the close of the last meeting in the Town Hall, as they were all congratulating the old man on the success of the day, he turned them on them saying, "Those are not the people I came thousands of miles to reach. Where were the drunkards and the prostitutes? Where were the lost sheep?" And exhausted as he must have been, he came to those to whom he had given his heart and his soul and his life...

Another meeting was announced. It would be held at midnight that same night, but this time at the Salvation Army hall, in a totally different part of the city. (Just picture one of our modern, high-paid, slick, professional evangelists doing something like that!) A Christian woman whose life was transformed by the events that night managed to get into the packed hall:

> And what a sight! Here gathered in the hundreds were the offscourings of the Sydney streets—prostitutes, drunks, opium sellers and users, in all their misery and lostness. And speaking to them was not the great leader of a world Army, a general of a great fighting force, but rather a tender father, a lover who opened his heart in compassion and love, to woo them back into the world of light and life.

*That* is the primary ministry of the Church! *That* is what God will anoint: passionate, brokenhearted, fervent, selfless, Jesus-exalting, winning of souls! As Booth himself implored his followers: "Go for souls! And go for the worst."

That will most certainly rock the boat.

*If there is anything of power in my ministry today, it is because God has all the adoration of my heart, all the power of my will, and all the influence of my life.*

William Booth

*Let the Holy Spirit fill every chamber of your heart; and so there will be no room for folly, or the world, or Satan, or the flesh.*

Robert Murray M'Cheyne

*The true follower of Christ will not ask, "If I embrace this truth, what will it cost me?" Rather he will say, "This is truth. God help me to walk in it, let come what may!"*

A.W. Tozer

*I'll spend my life to my latest moments in dens and caves of the earth, if the Kingdom of Christ may be advanced.*

David Brainerd

*Let fire, the cross, the letting out of beasts upon me, breaking of my bones, the tearing of my members, the grinding of my whole body, and the torments of the devils come upon me; so be it, [that] I may get Christ.*

Jeremiah Burroughs

*Hilarianus the [Roman] governor...said to me, "Have pity on your father's grey head; have pity on your infant son. Offer the sacrifice for the welfare of the emperors." "I will not," I retorted. "Are you a Christian?" said Hilarianus. And I said: "Yes, I am." When my father persisted in trying to dissuade me, Hilarianus ordered him thrown to the ground and beaten with a rod. I felt sorry for Father, just as if I myself had been beaten. Then Hilarianus passed sentence on all of us: We were condemned to [be publicly mauled and devoured] by the beasts, and we returned to prison in high spirits.... (Spoken by a 22-year-old nursing mother, shortly before her martyrdom.)*

Perpetua

*I have only one passion; it is He, He alone.*

Nicholas L. Zinzendorf

# Chapter Fourteen

# Radical Loyalty, Ruthless Love

Exodus 32 describes the story of the golden calf. Only several months before this tragic incident, the Israelites had been slaves in Egypt. With their own eyes they had seen the Lord's mighty hand and outstretched arm. They witnessed the signs and wonders, the plagues and judgments, the smiting of the firstborn and the parting of the sea. Then, just weeks before the events described in Exodus 32, they had seen the glory of God cover Mount Sinai, and all the people—every single one—heard the Almighty speak:

> I am the Lord your God, who brought you out of Egypt, out of the land of slavery. You shall have no other gods before Me. You shall not make for yourself an idol...for I, the Lord your God, am a jealous God.... (Ex. 20:2-5)

Ten commandments were given, and Moses ascended the mountain to meet with God for 40 days and 40 nights. He was caught up in a supernatural Presence, neither eating nor drinking the entire time. *He heard God audibly for almost six straight weeks.* But, as Exodus 32 records:

> When the people saw that Moses was so long in coming
> down from the mountain, they gathered around Aaron and
> said, "Come, make us gods who will go before us. As for
> this fellow Moses who brought us up out of Egypt, we don't
> know what has happened to him." (v. 1)

The Israelites made an idol! They made for themselves
another god. They violated the very first terms of the
covenant. They went from the exodus to apostasy in a matter of days. How utterly perverse and unfaithful. Isn't it almost unbelievable?

Then Moses came down from the mountain.

> When Moses approached the camp and saw the calf and the
> dancing, his anger burned and he threw the tablets out of his
> hands, breaking them to pieces at the foot of the mountain.
> And he took the calf they had made and burned it in the fire;
> then he ground it to powder, scattered it on the water and
> made the Israelites drink it. (Ex. 32:19-20)

Can you feel the indignation of Moses? Can you sense
the shock of his soul and the horror of his heart? He went
from intimacy to idolatry, communion to carnality, splen-
dor to sensuality, indescribable beauty to unspeakable
betrayal. Of course he felt holy anger and righteous passion. His heart burned with the fire of God and with fire
*for* God.

> Moses saw that the people were running wild and that Aaron
> had let them get out of control and so become a laugh-
> ingstock to their enemies. So he stood at the entrance to the
> camp and said, "Whoever is for the Lord, come to me." And
> all the Levites rallied to him. Then he said to them, "This is
> what the Lord, the God of Israel, says: 'Each man strap a
> sword to his side. Go back and forth through the camp from

one end to the other, *each killing his brother and friend and neighbor.*' " The Levites did as Moses commanded, and that day about three thousand of the people died. (Ex. 32:25-28)

That is the kind of radical loyalty God required in the Old Testament! *Kill your brother and friend and neighbor*—your own flesh and blood, your best friend you grew up with, or that helpful next-door neighbor you know so well—if they have betrayed the Lord. Otherwise their idolatry will destroy the whole community.

Then Moses said, "You have been set apart to the Lord today, for you were against your own sons and brothers, and He has blessed you this day." (Ex. 32:29)

There is a lesson here for us! There is a New Testament application for this Old Testament command. We must be just as loyal to the Lord as the Levites were. There is to be no competition in our loyalty to the Lord! Devotion to Him—to His character, His will and His Word—must *totally* override all our devotion to other people, other desires and other "gods." He wants nothing less than our *whole* heart, our *whole* soul, our *whole* mind.

In the Old Covenant, believers were called to exterminate the enemies of God by the sword. This has changed radically in the New Covenant.

"Put your sword back in its place," Jesus said to [Peter], "for all who draw the sword will die by the sword." (Matt. 26:52)

New Covenant believers are *not* called to take up the sword or gun against their spiritual enemies. Christian activism must *not* resort to violence. But we must *utterly exterminate* from our hearts every spiritual disloyalty, every hint of compromise, every thought that is against the glory of God. We must do violence to the works of darkness. We must *absolutely* side with the Light. That is how tenacious our allegiance to the Lord should be! That should be the norm for every believer.

Is that our level of devotion to God? Do we have that much hatred for sin? But that is what we are called to in the Spirit.

Be merciful to those who doubt [doubting can be a sign of weakness, not wickedness]; snatch others from the fire and save them; to others show mercy, mixed with fear—*hating even the clothing stained by corrupted flesh.* (Jude 22-23)

We are to come out of the hiding place (see Ps. 91) filled with holy passion for a hell-bound people, *totally identified* with the heart purpose of our God. His burden must become our burden, His perspective our perspective, His will our will. He must be our life. Anyone or anything else that would seek to entice our hearts to sin or try to pull us away from God must be absolutely rejected in no uncertain terms. "I am a servant of the Lord, and Him alone will I serve!" That is what is meant by radical loyalty.

It is the kind of loyalty that Jesus demands:

Do not suppose that I have come to bring peace to the earth. I did not come to bring peace, but a sword. For I have come to turn "a man against his father, a daughter against her mother, a daughter-in-law against her mother-in-law—a man's enemies will be the members of his own household." [Mic. 7:6] Anyone who loves his father or mother more than Me is not worthy of Me; anyone who loves his son or daughter more than Me is not worthy of Me; and anyone

who does not take his cross and follow Me is not worthy of
Me. (Matt. 10:34-38)

Everyone and everything else comes second. Jesus
comes first. In fact, He comes first and He comes last.
(Read Hebrews 12:2 and Revelation 1:17.) *There is no
room for anything that interferes with Him.*

Now please don't misunderstand me. I am not saying to
get rid of your unsaved spouse or to throw out your unbelieving parents. I am not counseling you to take on a
"holier than thou" attitude toward the church and the world.
But I *am* urging you—no, the Word is urging you—to be
so loyal to the Lord, to be so committed to Him, to be so
in love with Him, that you will never, ever betray Him;
never, ever turn on Him; never, ever side with sin; never,
ever compromise with the world; never, ever allow family,
friends or associates to come between you and your Master.

Love must be *sincere*. Hate what is evil; cling to what is
good. ... Never be lacking in zeal, but keep your spiritual
fervor, serving the Lord. (Rom. 12:9,11)

If we build ourselves up in our most holy faith by praying in the Holy Spirit (Jude 20), and if we keep ourselves
in God's love (Jude 21), then we will hate "even the clothing stained by corrupted flesh" (Jude 23). Then we can
challenge the world with holy mercy mixed with fear.

The problem with so many of us is we come to sinners
with a skin-deep righteousness. That is because we have an
ankle-deep relationship with God! We say the right words,
but conviction does not come. We use the right phrases, but
there is no depth. Even our quoting of Scripture often sounds

hollow. It is because we are not radically loyal! Our witness is wanting and our love is listless.

The remedy does not come cheaply. Listen to George Stormont, a friend and biographer of Smith Wigglesworth:

> The Lord does not pour compassion into us the way we pour gasoline into our cars. It is released in our spirits as we are filled with the Holy Spirit and dwell continually in the presence of Jesus. That means being filled with God. Wigglesworth's frequent prayer was to be emptied of self and filled with God.
>
> The mainspring of his compassion was to feel as Christ felt.

That is an all-encompassing, all-demanding call! But did the Lord ever ask anyone to love Him with half a heart? Did He ever retract the command to "love the Lord your God with all your heart and with all your soul and with all your mind and with all your strength" (Mark 12:30)?

Did Jesus ever demand anything less than everything? How much of you and me did His precious blood purchase? Are we paid for in full or only in part?

> ...You are not your own; you were bought at a price. Therefore honor God with your body. ... You were bought at a price; do not become slaves of men. (1 Cor. 6:19-20; 7:23)

Through the cross, the world has been crucified to us and we have been crucified to the world (Gal. 6:14). Let us live out this crucified life as if we were literally *nailed* to it: unshakably, immovably, unswervingly loyal to the Lord!

Listen to this wonderful quote recounted by Charles Spurgeon:

> I met in one of Samuel Rutherford's letters an extraordinary expression of the coals of divine wrath all falling on the head of Christ, so that not one might fall on his people. "And yet," says he, "if one of those coals should drop from his head on mine and utterly consume me, yet if I felt it was a part of the coals that fell on him, and I was bearing it for his sake and in communion with him, I would choose it for my heaven."

For Rutherford, Heaven was not the streets of gold or the sea of glass; nor was it the angelic choirs or the river of life. It was being in intimate relationship with the Son of God, partaking in His life as well as sharing in His pain and death. Paul too was so caught up with the Lord Jesus that he embraced "the fellowship of sharing in His sufferings" as well as "the power of His resurrection" (Phil. 3:10). This is the mentality of all whose hearts have been captivated by the beauty and glory of the King.

> Extremism should be the norm for a Christian. Every day as we watch the news, we see that sin is exceedingly sinful. It can be defeated only by exceeding love, hope, joy, and self-sacrifice. God Himself does not give with measure... (Richard Wurmbrand).

Wurmbrand relates a story well known by the Chinese church: After the jailed Chinese Christian, Rev. Fang-Cheng, has faithfully endured torture, he is brought before the interrogator once again. He notices a heap of rags in chains, huddled in a corner. It is his mother! Her hair has turned white, her complexion gray. Cheng, deeply shaken, is asked to recite the Ten Commandments and is stopped when he comes to "Honor your father and mother."

"Tell us what you know about your brethren in faith and I promise that tonight you and your mother will be free. You will be able to give her care and honor. Let me see now whether you really believe in God and wish to fulfill His commandment."

It is not easy to make a decision. Cheng turns to his mother: "Mommy, what shall I do?"

The mother answers, "I have taught you from childhood to love Christ and His holy church. Don't mind my suffering. Seek to remain faithful to the Savior and His little brethren. If you betray, you are no more my son."

That was the last time that Fang-Cheng saw his mother. The probability is that she died under torture.

That is radical loyalty in action! But there is something else we are called to. It can best be described as ruthless love.

If your very own brother, or your son or daughter, or the wife you love, or your closest friend [Don't read these words quickly! Think about these people carefully: "If your very own brother, or your son or daughter, or the wife you love, or your closest friend"] secretly entices you, saying, "Let us go and worship other gods" (gods that neither you nor your fathers have known, gods of the peoples around you, whether near or far, from one end of the land to the other), *do not yield to him or listen to him*…. (Deut. 13:6-8)

Many of us fall right there! We are seduced by human pressure and entrapped by earthly affection. The pull of people and the tug of the flesh sometimes overpower our half-hearted spiritual resolve. But the Lord doesn't just say, "Do not yield or listen." No. There's more.

...Show him no pity. [Remember to whom this refers!] Do not spare him or shield him. [Who of us wouldn't want to try to spare or shield someone we dearly loved? But the Lord says no!] You must certainly put him to death. *Your hand must be the first in putting him to death,* and then the hands of all the people. *Stone him to death,* because he tried to turn you away from the Lord your God, who brought you out of Egypt, out of the land of slavery. (Deut. 13:8-10)

That is ruthless love! "Your hand must be the first in putting him to death...because he tried to turn you away from the Lord your God." The moment anyone—our husband or wife whom we love so deeply; our dear, precious children who are the fruit of our own bodies; or our closest, most intimate friends—seek to turn us away from the Lord, *they become our spiritual enemies.* (Remember, though, we are to love our enemies, and we are never to harm them or seek to destroy them.)

Didn't Jesus identify *Satan* as the one who inspired Peter to say, "Lord, You will never go to the cross!" (See Matthew 16:21-22.)

...Get behind Me, Satan! [Jesus said to Peter.] You are a stumbling block to Me; you do not have in mind the things of God, but the things of men. (Matt. 16:23)

Shouldn't we recognize as satanic any suggestion that tells us not to take up *our* cross?

Of course, we are not to go around calling people "Satan" and delude ourselves into thinking that everyone who disagrees with us is our enemy. Nor are we to become paranoid, "we alone are the holy remnant" zealots who revel in always being right. That is both dangerous and hypocritical. But we are to have the same *attitude* that Deuteronomy 13 speaks of. We must love God enough that *if we had been Old Testament saints* and someone we dearly loved tried to entice us into idolatry, we would be willing to show them no pity, to not shield or protect them, to be the first ones to stone them to death out of our absolute allegiance to the Lord.

We can even take this one step further. As New Testament believers who have been redeemed (not from slavery in Egypt but from eternal damnation), who have been set free (not by a display of God's power that cost Him nothing but by the blood of His Son, which cost Him everything), how much more ruthless should our love be? How much deeper should our faithfulness be? The words of Peter, "Even if all fall away on account of You, I never will" and "Even if I have to die with You, I will never disown You" (Matt. 26:33,35) may have been presumptuous and rash. But they were commendable in terms of covenant love! How deep is our covenant love for the Lord?

The early church gloried in the story of the Martyrdom of Polycarp, the saintly old disciple of the apostle John who was one of the most beloved Christian leaders in Asia Minor. He was arrested by the Roman authorities and brought into a packed, giant stadium, the huge crowd hungry for his death. The proconsul said, "Revile Christ, and I will release you." Polycarp's reply was a classic:

> Eighty and six years have I served Him, and He has never done me wrong; how can I blaspheme Him, my King, who has saved me? I am a Christian.

So Polycarp gladly chose the flames, requesting that he not even be fastened to the stake. Even in the act of being burned alive, he would be steadfast! His heart was forever fixed. He would never deny the Lord. Jesus his Master had never wronged him, and he could not wrong his Lord. *Nor has Jesus ever wronged us.* Have we any reason to let Him down?

So what if they shoot us. So what if we lose everything. So what if it costs us our lives. Do we have any life outside of Him? Do we owe anyone else what we owe Him? Does anyone else truly own us, in the fullest sense of the word? And does anyone else pay what He pays: eternal life, unending joy, perfect peace, and "an inheritance that can never perish, spoil or fade—kept in heaven for you" (1 Pet. 1:4)?

No wonder Paul could say:

> I consider that our present sufferings [Paul was not speaking lightly here] are not worth comparing with the glory that will be revealed in us. (Rom. 8:18)

And William E. Simpson, a missionary who grew up in Tibet and China, never married, suffered great hardship, and was eventually murdered by a horde of Muslim army deserters, was not crazy when he wrote:

> All the trials, the loneliness, the heartache, the weariness and pain, the cold and fatigue of the long road, the darkness and discouragements, and all the bereavements, temptations and testings, seemed not worthy to be compared with the glory and joy of witnessing to this "glad tidings of great joy."

That is the biblical norm! That is an accurate assessment of reality, an acute analysis of what genuinely matters. That is truth. But it is quite a challenge! Could *we* ever say the same things?

The key is a closer, more intimate walk with the Lord. The key is deeper fellowship with the Father, deeper solidarity with the Son, deeper harmony with the Holy Spirit. It is the recognition that our Lord really is worthy of our all, that nothing makes more eternal sense than living absolutely for Him.

The God of Moses, the God of Paul, the God of Polycarp, the God of William Simpson, is still the same today. He still says, "Worship Me alone." He still says, "Have no other gods." His name is still Jealous (Ex. 34:14). He still demands radical loyalty. He still calls for ruthless love. He still deserves our all. As the hymn writer said:

> Jesus paid it all, all to Him I owe.
> Sin had a left a crimson stain;
> He washed it white as snow.

It's time we pay our debt.

*The early Christians knew that active faith in the Crucified and Risen Redeemer requires putting one's body on the line.*

Carl F. H. Henry

*Let no cross be considered too heavy to be borne in following Christ; no loss too great to be sustained for Christ; and no path too holy in going after Christ.*

James B. Taylor

*If the queen be pleased to release me, I will thank her; if she will imprison me, I will thank her; if she will burn me, I will thank her. (He was ultimately burned at the stake.)*

John Bradford

*I am the wheat of God and am ground by the teeth of the wild beasts, that I may be found the pure bread of God. (On the way to his martyrdom in Rome.)*

Ignatius of Antioch

*There was a day when I died, utterly died to my opinions, preferences, tastes, and will—died to the world, its approval or censure—died to the approval or blame even of my brethren and friends, and since then I have studied only to show myself approved unto God.*

George Mueller

*Many who are great in the sight of the Lord are living in cottages and hovels, and are scarcely known, unless to a few neighbors equally obscure.*

William Jay

# Chapter Fifteen

# Are You Willing to Lose Your Life?

Just for a moment, forget that you live in America. Forget about your home, your car and your possessions. Forget about your liberty and religious freedom. Come with me to China. Will you follow Jesus there?

Being a Christian in this communist land could cost you your life. It is very likely that you will be persecuted. You could well lose your job and your income. A prison term is not unlikely; torture is surely possible. You might never see your family again. The pressure will be intense, the hatred at times ferocious, the slander always present. Will you be a Christian in China?

Or go back 19 centuries to Rome. Will you join the believers in the catacombs, worshiping in secret and praying in the underground caves? Will you refuse to pledge allegiance to Caesar, even though informers are always near and your own family might betray you? Will you still tell others about your Lord?

But the situation in China and the catacombs is not abnormal. In fact, *in the time it has taken you to read this book, believers have probably been martyred.* (It is possible that believers will be martyred in the time it takes you to read just this chapter!) As Dietrich Bonhoeffer, the German theologian and pastor killed by the Nazis for plotting against Hitler, said, "When Christ calls a man, He bids him come and die." Will you come and die?

> Then Jesus said to His disciples, "If anyone would come after Me, he must deny himself and take up his cross and follow Me. For whoever wants to save his life will lose it, but whoever loses his life for Me will find it." (Matt. 16:24-25)

> I tell you the truth, unless a kernel of wheat falls to the ground and dies, it remains only a single seed. But if it dies, it produces many seeds. The man who loves his life will lose it, while the man who hates his life in this world will keep it for eternal life. (John 12:24-25)

What exactly did Jesus mean? Let's start with a totally literal interpretation: martyrdom. It is not impossible that following Jesus *here in the United States* could soon mean literal death. It is not impossible that some of us will be called on to seal our testimony with our blood. It is not unlikely that a righteous confrontation with a raging, ungodly mob will end with murder. (Our moral battle could soon become a mortal battle!) It is not improbable that there will be Stephens in our midst again. If *that* is what the gospel required, would we still follow the Lord?

*Willingness to be martyred provides an ideal starting point for the Christian life.* Consider what Jesus taught:

> Do not be afraid of those who kill the body but cannot kill
> the soul. Rather, be afraid of the One who can destroy both
> soul and body in hell. (Matt. 10:28)

In other words, don't be afraid of people. The worst they can do is kill you! They can only take your life. You are called to lose your life anyway! To be absent from the body means to be present with the Lord (2 Cor. 5:8 KJV). So what is there to fear? For the believer, death has lost its sting, for "whether we live or die, we belong to the Lord" (Rom. 14:8).

But we have fallen so far from biblical truth! For the average American believer, the concept of martyrdom is virtually incomprehensible. Instead of the call to "Come and die" we are used to the invitation to "come and dine" (John 21:12 KJV). As Thomas à Kempis wrote: "Many follow Jesus unto the breaking of bread; but few to the drinking of the cup of His passion."

*Today, in place of the old cross, we have the new cruise.* Christianity is primarily associated with earthly satisfaction, and the gospel is preached as if it existed for the purpose of personal fulfillment. Why meditate on our future heavenly dwelling when we're so at home here? Could the New Jerusalem be much flashier than some of our "monumental" gospel cathedrals?

A worldly mentality (i.e., a mentality oriented to this world) rules the day. What a contrast between the spirit of martyrdom and the spirit of the modern church! One endures the conflicts of this world by the power, life and joy of the world to come; the other enjoys this world.

We are more familiar with fashion than with fasting and more accustomed to pleasure than to passion. Some of our widely-advertised "prophets" hold $100-a-plate banquets—with personal words from the Lord to top off the feast—while others will bless your church for a guaranteed take of $10,000 or more. Even the presence of God can be purchased through one of our anointed "psalmists," as long as the price is right. (The right atmosphere, such as the finest luxury hotel, doesn't hurt either.)

We have entered the era of "marketing the church." But our whole methodology is faulty: The cross is not "user-friendly." It is "user-deadly"! Yet we think that we are soaring in the heights. The sad truth is we are often *too fat to fly*. The American church has been grounded!

How radically we have departed from the foundations of our faith! How deeply we have been deceived! It is time we turn our hearts back. It is time we recount the cost. *One of the chief things that holds us back from serving the Lord is our refusal to lose our lives.* We are always trying to hold on! Jesus calls us to let go.

Of course, not many of us will be martyred. (At least, not in the immediate future.) But all of us must renounce all claims to our lives. All of us must lose our rights. Then we can truly live!

Nobel Prize winner Alexander Solzhenytsin was imprisoned in Russia. He was separated from relatives and friends. He was taken from his career and vocation. He was stripped of his earthly possessions and treated as an insignificant nobody. Then, as the final insult, his *pencil* was confiscated. It was at that moment, Solzhenytsin said, that for the first time in his life, he became a totally free man. He had nothing more to lose! He had nothing more to be taken! There was nothing that anyone could hold over his head, nothing with which he could be threatened. In prison he found himself free.

Jesus calls us to be free! "Lose your life," He says. Then you will find it! "Die to this world," He urges. Then you will live! "Give up your reputation," He says. Then no one can take it! "Abandon your rights," He exhorts. Then all pressure will cease! You will be free to do His will. Nothing will be left to hold you back.

Yet so much of today's teaching goes against the way of the cross. Instead of encouraging believers to lose their rights, it instructs them to fight for their rights. (It is one thing to fight for moral and religious rights. It is another thing to fight for "personal rights," like the "right" to be angry with your selfish spouse, or the "right" to have a pity party when your friends reject you.) We are a generation that has emphasized preservation of self instead of denial of self, and catering to the flesh instead of crucifying it. That is not the biblical way!

> For it is commendable if a man bears up under the pain of unjust suffering because he is conscious of God. But how is it to your credit if you receive a beating for doing wrong and endure it? But if you suffer for doing good and you endure it, this is commendable before God. To this you were called, because Christ suffered for you, leaving you an example, that you should follow in His steps. (1 Pet. 2:19-21)

Yes, there are many dimensions to losing our lives!

We are called to love our enemies, to bless those who curse us, to pray for those who mistreat us, and to take an absolute stance of non-retaliation (Luke 6:27-29). That is part of dying to self. We must overcome evil with good (Rom. 12:21).

Our emotional "lusts" must also be denied. Bitterness is forbidden. Morbid moping is out. We must rid ourselves of anger, rage, malice and slander (Col. 3:8). Such are improper for God's holy people (Eph. 5:1-12). And we must speak out when there has been sin (Luke 17:3-4), like it or not. The brash person must become meek. The timid one must become bold. Death to the will of the flesh! Are you still willing to follow along?

"But I'd rather not witness to my neighbor." Then lose your life and obey the Lord! "My preference is not to attend the all-night prayer meeting." Since when did the Lord ask for our preference? "My flesh really doesn't want to fight for the unborn." Then crucify it and be equipped by the Spirit of our God. Our only "right" is to please the Lord, and what a glorious right it is! But there's still more to our call.

*We must die to our reputation.* The brilliant Saul of Tarsus was arrested, beaten, whipped, mocked, called crazy, and stoned. One time he escaped with his life by being lowered in a basket from a window in the city wall (2 Cor. 11:32-33). So much for being a professional evangelist! Oxford scholar John Wesley was pelted with rocks, rotten fruit, and dead cats. The once popular Charles Finney was often burned in effigy. It was because they were identified with Jesus. Are we also identified with Him? Do people associate Jesus with *us*?

> And so Jesus also suffered outside the city gate to make the people holy through His own blood. Let us, then, go to Him outside the camp, bearing the disgrace He bore. For here we do not have an enduring city, but we are looking for the city that is to come. (Heb. 13:12-14)

Will we also bear His disgrace?

> I would lead Hallelujah Bands and be a damn fool in the eyes of the world to save souls (Catherine Booth).

Is that the spirit we have? Would we be willing to march in such overt gospel displays, if our unbelieving friends, neighbors, relatives or employers were watching? May God open our eyes to reality!

Who cares about the opinion of the world? Why be moved by the secular media? Why be influenced by those who are spiritually lost? Why be held back by mere flesh and blood? God's eternal perspective is the only one that counts. In His sight, the proud professor is a fool and the simple saint is wise. That's why Paul could say, "I am not ashamed of the gospel" (Rom. 1:16) in spite of the disdain of the intellectuals and the scorn of the religious establishment. Can we say that we are not ashamed? Reputation must be nailed to the cross!

But there is another aspect to the crucified life. It is abandoning the right to self-determination.

> If we are to be in fellowship with Him we must deliberately go through the annihilation, not of glory, but of our former right to ourselves in every shape and form. Until this inner

martyrdom is gone through, temptation will always take us unawares (Oswald Chambers).

Taking back our lives is equivalent to robbing God!

The old man and his plans are dead. And dead men have no future. Only resurrected men have a future. We have been raised in Him! *Only dead men can be raised.*

> Since, then, *you have been raised with Christ,* set your hearts on things above, where Christ is seated at the right hand of God. Set your minds on things above, not on earthly things. *For you died,* and your life is now hidden with Christ in God. When Christ, who is your life, appears, then you also will appear with Him in glory. (Col. 3:1-4)

That describes the normal Christian life. We do not live out the rest of our earthly days for evil human desires, but rather for the will of God (1 Pet. 4:2). That is why Jesus died!

> And He died for all, that those who live should no longer live for themselves *but for Him who died for them and was raised again.* (2 Cor. 5:15)

Deeply engraved on the heart of every believer should be these words: "I live for the will of God. I have no will outside of His!" It is *to that* we have been saved. So shall it be for all time:

> No longer will there be any curse. The throne of God and of the Lamb will be in the city, *and His servants will serve Him.* (Rev. 22:3)

That is our eternal, blessed call!

We must come to grips with the fact that we are God's servants, that our lives belong to Him, and that He has the absolute right to send us anywhere, use us any way, and tell us to do anything at anytime. We did not sign a conditional contract with the Lord!

Of course, doing His will is glorious. He fulfills and blesses, the rewards are great, and all His ways are life. But the road to life is the path of the cross, and total victory can come only after full surrender. Are you still holding on, or are you willing to live *or* die for the Lord, to go *or* stay for Jesus, to pay *or* pray, to speak *or* be silent, to unconditionally yield to Him? Does anything hold you back? Are you ready to be enlisted? Are you listening for the Master's command—whatever that command may be?

Remember the wise words of missionary Jim Elliot, who was speared to death with his team by the Auca Indians as these missionaries sought to reach those poor sinners with the message of the love of God:

> He is no fool to lose what he cannot keep to gain what he cannot lose.

What is it you want to gain? Do you really have anything to lose? Take up your cross and follow the Lord. You will never regret that you did! Just ask Jim Elliot when you see him; that is, if your eyes can take all the glory:

> Those who are wise will shine like the brightness of the heavens, and those who lead many to righteousness, like the stars for ever and ever. (Dan. 12:3)

May *you* shine like the sun on that day, when death will give way to life. Forever.

*Let the devil choose his way; God is a match for him at every weapon. The devil and his whole council are but fools to God; nay, their wisdom foolishness.*

William Gurnall

*What a difference in the men who go into battle intending to conquer if they can, and those who go into battle intending to conquer.*

D.L. Moody

*A coward heart will not do for the day of battle; a doubting spirit will not stand in conflict.*

C.H. Mackintosh

*A true Christian is unique. He stands alone. He supersedes all who have gone before. He will not have a successor. He is man at his best, and God's best effort for mankind.*

John G. Lake

*We are a supernatural people; born again by a supernatural birth; we wage a supernatural fight and are taught by a supernatural teacher; led by a supernatural captain to assured victory.*

J. Hudson Taylor

*On the following words I staked everything, and they never failed, "Lo, I am with you always, even unto the end of the world."*

David Livingstone

# Chapter Sixteen

# Forward March!

The children of Israel had their backs to the wall. The Egyptian army was pursuing them, gaining ground by the minute. The sea was before them, cutting off their path.

They were terrified and cried out to the Lord. (Ex. 14:10b)

Then the Lord said something extraordinary to his servant Moses:

...Why are you crying out to Me? Tell the Israelites to move on. (Ex. 14:15)

Paraphrased in The Living Bible, this verse says:

...Quit praying and get the people moving! Forward, march!

*"Moses, children of Israel, why are you crying out to Me?"* Imagine what Moses must have thought. "Is God playing some kind of cruel joke? The Egyptian army, with horses and chariots, is about to slaughter us, and You ask, 'Why are you crying out to Me?' Our women and children will die by drowning or by the sword, and You ask, 'Why are you crying out to Me?' " But the Lord says, "Forward march!"

There is a word here for the Church! Can you see it written between the lines?

Our walk is a walk of faith. We pray by faith and we obey by faith. Our Captain is completely invisible, yet our eyes are fastened on Him: "...[Moses] persevered because he saw Him who is invisible. ... Therefore...let us run with perseverance the race marked out for us. Let us fix our eyes on Jesus..." (Heb. 11:27; 12:1-2)—and when He says, "Forward march!"—we march! Our Commander has cleared the way. That means the power is there, the anointing is there, the authority is there, the answer is there. Final victory is assured. But we must arise and act! God's blessing is on those who go.

Remember what the risen Lord said:

> ...*All authority* in heaven and on earth has been given to Me. [Read those words again slowly and out loud, meditating on every one. There is *no* authority against Jesus, no greater power, no force that can threaten.] *Therefore go* and make disciples of all nations.... (Matt. 28:18-19)

Now is the hour to go!

For years we have petitioned the Lord in prayer, seeking Him for revival and renewal, beseeching Him to send the rain and the fire. And beseech Him and petition Him we must! We must press in and pray even more. We must seek Him until every last promise is fulfilled. But, there is a time to pray and wait, and there is a time to pray and act. *Now is the time to act.*

"Why are you crying out to Me?" the Lord asks. He knows that the enemy is chasing us, and that the odds are entirely impossible. He knows that the obstacles before us are immovable and impenetrable. But there is something else He knows. If our heart is pure, if our life is right, if we live to do His will, if we wait before Him in faith, if He is our Lord and King—then His glory resides in us! His power lives in us! His Word abides in us! His Spirit inhabits us! "Forward march!" He says, equipped with the weapons of God. *He fights for those who march by faith, heeding only the divine command.*

To Moses, God said:

And you lift up your rod and hold out your arm over the sea *and split it,* so that the Israelites may march into the sea on dry ground. (Ex. 14:16, New Jewish Version)

"Moses, *you* split the sea!" The Hebrew is in the imperative. This is an order from the Lord!

"Moses, don't wait for something new to happen. You already have the rod of God. Now use it as I command. Raise it and part the sea. Make the dry land appear!"

Listen to the marching orders Jesus gave to His disciples:

"As you go, preach this message: "The kingdom of heaven is near." Heal the sick, raise the dead, cleanse those who have leprosy, drive out demons. Freely you have received, freely give. (Matt. 10:7-8)

"Disciples, I've given My authority to you!" (See Matthew 10:1.) "Now *you* go, *you* preach, *you* heal the sick. (That's right, *you* heal the sick!) *You* raise the dead, *you* cleanse the lepers, *you* drive out demons."

That's what Jesus was saying! And that's what He is saying to us: To the extent that we have received, we are obligated, and privileged, to give. And although we are nowhere near fully restored, we are commanded to give what we have. We are to be just like the widow at Zarepath (1 Kin. 17). When she gave the little she had, the Lord removed all her lack. She was never without God's supply.

So don't sit back and complain. Don't whimper and wail, murmur and groan. Get up, believe, and act! Pour out what you have and grace will pour in. God is calling His Church to march forth!

*March forth for the glory of God* like William C. Burns, the Scottish revivalist who gave his life for Chinese souls. When asked if he was going to that far-off land to convert the heathen, he replied, "I am going to China to glorify God!"

*March forth and catch men,* like John Geddie, the pioneer Presbyterian missionary to the South Seas:

> On a tablet in a large church seating 1,000 people this inscription was placed in memory of John Geddie: "When he landed in 1848 there were no Christians here; when he left in 1872 there were no heathen."

*March forth for righteousness and morality* like William Wilberforce, the British aristocrat who gave himself sacrificially to fight against slavery. His vision was impossible. Society was against him. History was against him. Common prejudices were against him. *But God was for him.*

This is an excerpt from the letter that 88-year-old John Wesley wrote to the 31-year-old Wilberforce in 1791, just four days before Wesley's death:

Unless the divine power has raised you up to be as Athanasius against the world [Athanasius stood his ground for the truth against what seemed like a tidal wave of opposition], I see not how you can go through your glorious enterprise, in opposing that execrable villainy, which is the scandal of religion, of England, and of human nature. Unless God raise you up for this very thing, you will be worn out by the opposition of men and devils. But, "if God be for you, who can be against you?" Are all of them together stronger than God? O "be not weary in well doing!" Go on, in the name of God and in the power of His might, till even the American slavery (the vilest that ever saw the sun) shall vanish away before it.

People of God: Forward march!

March forth with clean hands and an honest heart. March forth with steadfast faith and a will of steel. March forth with holy conduct and righteous deeds. March forth with compassion and kindness, clothed with the mercy of the Lord. March forth with the name of Jesus on your lips and His praises alive in your soul. March forth and conquer for Him!

Conquer the lies of darkness and the deceptions of the enemy. Conquer the demons and disease, the unseen terrorists that dominate and destroy. Conquer hopelessness and despair, fear and dismay. Conquer by the Spirit of God. Do it for His glory, for the One you love. Do it for this sin-smitten race for whom Jesus died. Do it out of honor for Him!

Then, be honest with yourself. We will not save the whole planet. We will not rule the world in this age. We will not eradicate wickedness. We will not wipe out sickness and death. *But we will make an impact for the Lord*—and what an eternal difference it will make! We will effect radical change! And some generation (why not ours?) will live to see the day when Jesus our Savior returns. Then this Scripture will come to pass:

> The kingdom of this world has become the kingdom of our Lord and of His Christ, and He will reign for ever and ever. (Rev. 11:15b)

Not long after, the day will come when "there will be no more death or mourning or crying or pain, for the old order of things has passed away" (Rev. 21:4), never again to return!

Therefore, in light of eternity, in light of what Jesus has done for us, in light of the fact that we have but one short life to live on this earth, one fleeting opportunity to repay our infinite debt of gratitude, one chance to impact humanity for God, in light of all this, let us take heart and march forth. The battle has already been won!

Listen one last time to the words of William Booth, as the Salvation Army General marshalled his troops for war:

> On to Calvary! On to death for the world! Let us not refuse the smiters! No halting! No rest! On, suffering, sorrowing, weeping, dying for God and men, till the hosts of hell fly from their last defence, and we march on over a burning world into everlasting glory!

People of God, arise! *It's time to rock the boat.*

# References

Many of the quotations cited at the beginning of each chapter were taken from the compilation of Stephen L. Hill, *On Earth as It Is in Heaven: A Classic Bible Reading Guide* (available by writing to P.O. Box 2050, Lindale, TX, 75771). This little book consists of the famous daily Bible reading plan of Robert Murray M'Cheyne, introduced each day by a quotation selected by Hill. Other sources of quotations which I utilized include: Harry Verploegh, ed., *Oswald Chambers: The Best from All His Books*, Vols. I and II (Oliver Nelson, 1987, 1989); Tom Carter, ed., *Spurgeon at His Best* (Baker, 1988); *Carl Henry at His Best: A Lifetime of Quotable Thoughts* (Multnomah, 1989). Other quotes were taken from miscellaneous volumes in my study. Only citations within the chapters themselves are identified in the notes that follow.

Special Note: I have *not* cited by name the pastors, teachers and authors whose writings I challenge and with whom I disagree. This has been done for two reasons: First, there is a "witch-hunting" mentality in the Body today that is both dangerous and divisive. If I differ with a fellow believer by name over *one issue*, the tendency in many circles is to brand this person as "heretical" in every issue. This is harmful and immature. Second, in a scholarly study with ample footnotes and documentation, it is proper and correct to interact critically with different authors and teachers, citing name and publication in detail. However, because this book is popular in style, I felt it would be better to center on issues instead of personalities. If you recognize the authors whose views I challenge, then by all means read their books prayerfully, and where necessary, separate the wheat from the chaff.

Page 5—Andrew Bonar, *Memoir and Remains of R. M. M'Cheyne* (repr., Banner of Truth, 1987), 11.

Page 5—Samuel Logan Brengle, *When the Holy Ghost is Come* (repr., Salvation Army, 1982), 108-09.

Page 14—Arthur Wallis, *In the Day of Thy Power* (repr., Cityhill/Christian Literature Crusade, 1990), 87.

Page 28—James A. Stewart, *Evangelism* (repr., Revival Literature, n.d.), 34.

Page 31—Charles Spurgeon, cited in Stewart, *Evangelism*, 44.

Page 33—*Theological Dictionary of the New Testament* (ET G.W. Bromiley; Eerdmans, 1967), 4:1000 (article by J. Behm).

Pages 33-34—A.T. Robertson, *Word Pictures in the New Testament* (repr., Baker, n.d.), 3:34.

Page 34—*New International Dictionary of New Testament Theology*, ed. Colin Brown (Zondervan, 1986), 1:358 (article by J. Goetzmann).

Page 38— William Booth, cited in Stewart, *Evangelism*, 31.

Page 50—A. Skevington Wood, *The Burning Heart. John Wesley: Evangelist* (Bethany, 1978), 148.

Page 50—John Worthington, cited in Wood, *The Burning Heart*, 148.

Pages 50-51—John Wesley, cited in Wood, *The Burning Heart*, 150-51, 149.

Pages 56-57—John Preston, John Bunyan and Richard Baxter, all cited in Leland Ryken, *Worldly Saints: The Puritans as They Really Were* (Zondervan, 1986), 91, 107.

Page 58—David Wilkerson, printed message.

Page 68—The young Chinese man was quoted by Jonathan and Rosalind Goforth, *Miracle Lives of China* (repr., Bethel, 1988).

Page 70— Edward N. Gross, *Christianity Without a King: The Results of Abandoning Christ's Lordship* (Brentwood Christian Press, 1992), 18-19.

Pages 75-76—Jonathan Goforth, *When the Spirit's Fire Swept Korea* (Bethel, n.d.), 8-9.

Page 77—A.T. Robertson, *Word Pictures*, 3:34.

Page 78—Walter Phillips, cited in Jonathan Goforth, *By My Spirit* (Bethel, 1983), 41-42.

Page 78—Jonathan Goforth, *When the Spirit's Fire Swept Korea*, 10.

Pages 78-79—This description of William Booth's ministry was taken from Minnie Lindsay Carpenter, *William Booth* (Schmul, 1986), 28.

Page 79—Catherine Booth, cited in Carpenter, *William Booth*, 44.

Pages 79-80—William C. Burns, cited in James Alexander Stewart, *William Chalmers Burns; Robert Murray Mc-Cheyne: Biographical Sketches* (Revival Literature, n.d.), 27.

Pages 80-82—Jonathan Goforth, *When the Spirit's Fire Swept Korea*, 10, 14-15, 25.

Page 88—J.C. Ryle, *Holiness: Its Nature, Hindrances, Difficulties, and Roots* (repr., Evangelical Press, 1991), 22.

Page 91—John Wesley, *The Works of John Wesley* (repr., Baker, 1986), 1:103-04.

Page 94—Alexander Maclaren, cited in J. Gregory Mantle, *The Counterfeit Christ and Other Sermons* (Christian Publications, n.d.), 36.

Page 108—Jonathan Edwards, cited in John Gerstner, *Heaven and Hell: Jonathan Edwards on the Afterlife* (Ligonier/Baker, 1991), 61.

Pages 115-16—T. Austin Sparks, *The School of Christ* (1964; repr., World Challenge, n.d.), 9.

Page 122—Oswald Chambers, *My Utmost for His Highest* (repr., Barbour and Co., n.d.), 253 (September 9th).

Page 126—Smith Wigglesworth, cited in Jack Hywel-Davies, *The Life of Smith Wigglesworth: One Man, One Holy Passion* (Servant, 1988), 120.

Pages 129-30—A.W. Tozer, cited in James L. Snyder, *The Pursuit of God: The Life of A.W. Tozer* (Christian Publications, 1991), 15.

Page 135—John Wesley, cited in Leonard Ravenhill, *Why Revival Tarries* (Bethany, 1959), 16.

Page 136—For the Oswald Chambers quote, see Michael L. Brown, *Whatever Happened to the Power of God?* (Destiny Image, 1991), 23-31.

Page 137—K. P. Yohannan, *The Road to Reality: Coming Home to Jesus from the Unreal World* (Creation House, 1988), 26.

Page 137—James Gilmour, cited in Ravenhill, *Why Revival Tarries*, 36.

Page 140—Thomas Goodwin, cited in Iaian H. Murray, *The Puritan Hope: Revival and the Interpretation of Prophecy* (Banner of Truth, 1971), 103.

Pages 151-52 The account of William Booth in Australia is taken from Charles Talmadge, ed., *How to Preach: William Booth* (repr., Salvation Army, 1979), xiv-xvi.

Page 160—George Stormont, *Smith Wigglesworth: A Man Who Walked with God* (Harrison House, 1989), 29.

Page 161—Charles Spurgeon, from *The Best of Spurgeon*, 201-02 (#1387).

Pages 161-62—Richard Wurmbrand, "The Voice of the Martyrs" (Newsletter), January 1993, 1-2.

Page 165—William E. Simpson, cited in James and Marti Hefley, *By their Blood: Christian Martyrs of the 20th Century* (Baker, 1979), 147.

Page 170—Dietrich Bonhoeffer, *The Cost of Discipleship* (Macmillian, 1963), 99.

Pages 175-76—Oswald Chambers, from *The Best From All His Books*, 2:191

Page 182—William C. Burns, cited in Stewart, *Biographical Sketches*, 8.

Page 182— The memorial to Presbyterian missionary John Geddie is cited in Ravenhill, *Why Revival Tarries*, 156.

Page 183—John Wesley's letter to William Wilberforce, *The Works of John Wesley*, 13:153.

Page 184—William Booth, cited in Talmadge, ed., *How to Preach*, xv, xvi.

# *Destiny Image*
# Revival Books

# Destiny Image
# Revival Books

## IMAGES OF REVIVAL
*by Richard and Kathryn Riss.*

"Revival" means many things to many people. But what is real revival actually like? In this brief overview, the authors examine the many images of revivals that have occurred throughout the years. God's moves upon His people are exciting and sometimes unexpected. Learn how revival could come to your community!

Paperback Book, 182p. ISBN 1-56043-687-5 Retail $8.99

## SHARE THE FIRE
*by Guy Chevreau.*

Do you panic when you hear the word *evangelism*? Do you feel awkward "forcing" your opinions on another? All that changes when God abundantly and freely fills you with His Spirit! In *Share the Fire* you'll learn how God has intended evangelism to be: a bold and free work of Christ in you and through you!

Paperback Book, 182p. ISBN 1-56043-688-3 Retail $8.99

## THE CHURCH OF THE 3RD MILLENNIUM
*by Marc Dupont.*

Uncontrollable laughter, violent shaking, falling "under the Spirit"—can these things really be from God? Using examples from the ministries of Elijah, John the Baptist, and Jesus Himself, Marc Dupont shows that God often moves in ways that challenge traditional religious views or habits; He "offends the mind in order to reveal the heart." God's end-time Church shouldn't be satisfied with the status quo. We need to reach for more of God's Spirit—and not be surprised when He gives it to us!

Paperback Book, 182p. ISBN 1-56043-194-6 Retail $8.99

## Available at your local Christian bookstore.

### Internet: http://www.reapernet.com

Prices subject to change without notice.